CAMBRIDGE SCHOOL

Shakespeare

Twelfth Night

Edited by Rex Gibson

Series Editor: Rex Gibson
Director, Shakespeare and Schools Project

CAMBRIDGE
UNIVERSITY PRESS

PUBLISHED BY THE PRESS SYNDICATE OF THE UNIVERSITY OF CAMBRIDGE
The Pitt Building, Trumpington Street, Cambridge CB2 1RP, United Kingdom

CAMBRIDGE UNIVERSITY PRESS
The Edinburgh Building, Cambridge CB2 2RU, United Kingdom
40 West 20th Street, New York, NY 10011–4211, USA
10 Stamford Road, Oakleigh, Melbourne 3166, Australia

First published 1993
Fifth printing 1998

Printed in the United Kingdom at the University Press, Cambridge

A catalogue record for this book is available from the British Library

Library of Congress Cataloguing in Publication data applied for

ISBN 0 521 43536 6 paperback

Designed by Richard Morris, Stonesfield Design
Picture research by Callie Kendall

pp. 8, 44, 118, 125*l*, Angus McBean/print by Shakespeare Centre Library, Stratford-upon-Avon; pp. 12, 56, 62, 90, 125*b*, Morris Newcombe; pp. 22, 102, 125*tr*, 163, Shakespeare Centre Library, Stratford-upon-Avon: Joe Cocks Studio Collection; p. 35, Zoë Dominic; pp. 38, 138, Shakespeare Centre Library, Stratford-upon-Avon: Tom Holte Theatre Photographic Collection; p. 69, Clive Barda/Performing Arts Library; p. 70, Mary Evans Picture Library; pp. 78, 148, Reg Wilson; pp. 84, 125*tc*, Donald Cooper © Photostage; p. 109, *Stratford-upon-Avon Herald*/print by Shakespeare Centre Library, Stratford-upon-Avon; p. 153, Koninklijk Museum voor Schone Kunsten; p. 155, Earl Young/Robert Harding Picture Library; p. 167, Contemporary Films Ltd/print by British Film Institute.

Contents

Cambridge School Shakespeare

This edition of *Twelfth Night* is part of the *Cambridge School Shakespeare* series. Like every other play in the series, it has been specially prepared to help all students in schools and colleges.

This *Twelfth Night* aims to be different from other editions of the play. It invites you to bring the play to life in your classroom, hall or drama studio through enjoyable activities that will increase your understanding. Actors have created their different interpretations of the play over the centuries. Similarly, you are encouraged to make up your own mind about *Twelfth Night*, rather than having someone else's interpretation handed down to you.

Cambridge School Shakespeare does not offer you a cut-down or simplified version of the play. This is Shakespeare's language, filled with imaginative possibilities. You will find on every left-hand page: a summary of the action, an explanation of unfamiliar words, a choice of activities on Shakespeare's language, characters and stories.

Between each act and in the pages at the end of the play, you will find notes, illustrations and activities. These will help to increase your understanding of the whole play.

There are a large number of activities to give you the widest choice to suit your own particular needs. Please don't think you have to do every one. Choose the activities that will help you most.

This edition will be of value to you whether you are studying for an examination, reading for pleasure, or thinking of putting on the play to entertain others. You can work on the activities on your own or in groups. Many of the activities suggest a particular group size, but don't be afraid to make up larger or smaller groups to suit your own purposes.

Although you are invited to treat *Twelfth Night* as a play, you don't need special dramatic or theatrical skills to do the activities. By choosing your activities, and by exploring and experimenting, you can make your own interpretations of Shakespeare's language, characters and stories. Whatever you do, remember that Shakespeare wrote his plays to be acted, watched and enjoyed.

Rex Gibson

This edition of *Twelfth Night* uses the text of the play established by Elizabeth Story Donno in *The New Cambridge Shakespeare*.

List of characters

Illyria

The Duke's court
ORSINO, Duke of Illyria
VALENTINE, a courtier
CURIO, a courtier
Musicians
Lords
Officers

The Countess's household
OLIVIA, a countess
SIR TOBY BELCH, her uncle
MALVOLIO, her steward
FESTE, her fool
MARIA, her gentlewoman
FABIAN, a servant

A PRIEST
A SEA CAPTAIN

The visitors

VIOLA, later called Cesario
SEBASTIAN, her twin brother
SIR ANDREW AGUECHEEK, suitor to Olivia
ANTONIO, a friend to Sebastian
Sailors

The action of the play takes place in Illyria

Orsino calls for music to feed his hunger for love. He reflects that love is like the sea, absorbing and devaluing every other experience. He claims to be completely obsessed by his love for Olivia.

1 Love or infatuation? (in pairs)

The opening lines of *Twelfth Night* suggest the play will be much about love. But what sort of love? You will find various expressions of love throughout the play. Here's the first sight of one lover: Count Orsino, Duke of Illyria. Many people believe he's not a true lover at all, just indulging the idea of love. One student described him as 'Not really in love with anything except the thought of love. You can tell it from the way he talks.'

Well, can you? Try one or more of these activities to discover what you think about Orsino:

a Speak lines 1–15 in different ways: for example, thoughtfully, sadly, loudly as if to a public meeting. Then talk together about what you think is the most appropriate tone of voice for Orsino.

b In line 4, Orsino asks for a musical refrain to be repeated ('That strain again'). But by line 7 he has heard enough, so he tells the musicians to stop playing. How do you think they feel about their master's quick change of mood? One person reads Orsino's lines, pausing at each punctuation mark. In the pauses, the other person, as a musician, comments on what Orsino says.

c Advise the actor playing Orsino how to speak line 7: 'Enough; no more.' For example, would you wish to make the audience laugh?

2 Staging the opening (in small groups)

How would you present these opening minutes to an audience? Talk together about set, costumes, actors and the general impression you would wish to create of Orsino's court. What kind of music would you use?

---

surfeiting over-filled
That strain again play that again
validity and pitch high value
falls into abatement is lessened
fancy love

high fantastical intensely
  imaginative
hart male deer
pestilence plague
fell savage

Twelfth Night

or What You Will

ACT 1 SCENE 1
Orsino's palace

Music. Enter ORSINO, *Duke of Illyria*, CURIO, *and other Lords*

ORSINO If music be the food of love, play on;
　　　Give me excess of it, that surfeiting,
　　　The appetite may sicken and so die.
　　　That strain again, it had a dying fall;
　　　O it came o'er my ear like the sweet sound　　　　5
　　　That breathes upon a bank of violets,
　　　Stealing and giving odour. Enough; no more.
　　　'Tis not so sweet now as it was before.
　　　O spirit of love, how quick and fresh art thou,
　　　That, notwithstanding thy capacity,　　　　10
　　　Receiveth as the sea. Nought enters there,
　　　Of what validity and pitch soe'er,
　　　But falls into abatement and low price
　　　Even in a minute. So full of shapes is fancy,
　　　That it alone is high fantastical.　　　　15
CURIO Will you go hunt, my lord?
ORSINO　　　　　　　　　　What, Curio?
CURIO The hart.
ORSINO Why so I do, the noblest that I have.
　　　O when mine eyes did see Olivia first,
　　　Methought she purged the air of pestilence;　　　　20
　　　That instant was I turned into a hart,
　　　And my desires like fell and cruel hounds
　　　E'er since pursue me.

Enter VALENTINE

　　　How now, what news from her?

3

*Valentine tells of Olivia's vow to mourn her dead brother for seven years.
Orsino says that this reveals how she will love him totally. Viola,
landed safely after shipwreck, fears for her brother's life.*

1 First news of Olivia (in pairs)

Work out from lines 26–32 just what Olivia has vowed to do. Then
make a list of words which describe your first impression of Olivia.

2 Just like a man!

Orsino thinks that if Olivia can go to such lengths just for love of a
brother, she will be completely obsessed when she falls in love with
him. Orsino sees himself becoming 'one selfsame king' of Olivia's
'sweet perfections', filling her sexual desire, thought and feeling
('liver, brain and heart').

Imagine that lines 33–41 are a mirror. As you read them, admire
yourself in that 'mirror', combing your hair and preening. Try it
several times, then think about how the activity adds to your view of
Orsino.

3 Scene shifting (in small groups)

In modern productions of Shakespeare's plays, each scene flows
swiftly into the next. There are no long delays for elaborate scene-
shifting. Work out how you would transfer the audience in imagination from Orsino's palace in Scene 1 to the sea-coast in Scene 2.
Present your solution as a design or in writing. Would you use the
musicians to help your plan?

4 Illyria = Elysium?

Notice how 'Elysium' (heaven, a peaceful, welcoming place) echoes
'Illyria'. Do you think Shakespeare intended this echo to create the
impression of a friendly, dream-like country?

---

element sky
seven years' heat seven summers
a cloistress a nun secluded from
  the world
eye-offending brine bitter tears
season preserve

rich golden shaft Cupid's arrow of
  love
bowers leafy, secluded places
Perchance (line 5) perhaps
perchance (line 6) by good fortune

VALENTINE So please my lord, I might not be admitted,
    But from her handmaid do return this answer: 25
    The element itself, till seven years' heat,
    Shall not behold her face at ample view;
    But like a cloistress she will veilèd walk,
    And water once a day her chamber round
    With eye-offending brine; all this to season   30
    A brother's dead love, which she would keep fresh
    And lasting, in her sad remembrance.
ORSINO O she that hath a heart of that fine frame
    To pay this debt of love but to a brother,
    How will she love, when the rich golden shaft   35
    Hath killed the flock of all affections else
    That live in her; when liver, brain, and heart,
    These sovereign thrones, are all supplied and filled
    Her sweet perfections with one selfsame king!
    Away before me to sweet beds of flowers: 40
    Love-thoughts lie rich when canopied with bowers.

                                Exeunt

ACT I   SCENE 2
The sea-coast of Illyria

Enter VIOLA, a CAPTAIN, and Sailors

VIOLA What country, friends, is this?
CAPTAIN This is Illyria, lady.
VIOLA And what should I do in Illyria?
    My brother, he is in Elysium.
    Perchance he is not drowned: what think you, sailors?   5
CAPTAIN It is perchance that you yourself were saved.
VIOLA O my poor brother! And so perchance may he be.

The Captain tells Viola that her brother may also have survived the shipwreck. He describes Orsino, and explains that Olivia's grief for her brother's death has made her a recluse.

1 'Arion on the dolphin's back' (in small groups)

The Captain compares Sebastian's possible escape from shipwreck with that of Arion, a legendary Greek musician. Arion leapt overboard to escape sailors who wished to murder him. A dolphin, enchanted by Arion's music, carried him safely to shore. The Captain's story gives Viola hope.

Some stage productions show Sebastian's struggle to survive. Imagine you are directing the play, and want the audience to see what happens to Sebastian. How will you present lines 11–17? Line 16 ('hold aquaintance') probably means that Sebastian managed to keep afloat quite well – like someone holding their own in a conversation.

2 'He was a bachelor then' (in pairs)

Suggest possible reasons for Viola's comment about Orsino: 'He was a bachelor then' (line 29). Talk together about what the remark implies about her character. How do you think she says the line?

3 'What great ones do, the less will prattle of'

The Captain's words (line 33) anticipate the modern-day paparazzi (photographers who specialise in spying on famous people like royalty and pop stars). They supply the pictures and stories which provide millions of 'the less' (ordinary people) with an endless source of rumour and gossip. Make a collection from newspapers and magazines to illustrate the line.

---

driving drifting
provident full of foresight
unfoldeth to encourages
The like of him that he too
  survived
very late recently

murmur rumour, gossip
abjured rejected, renounced
Till I . . . estate is! until the time is
  ripe to reveal my true identity
compass achieve, bring about
suit advances

CAPTAIN True, madam, and to comfort you with chance,
        Assure yourself, after our ship did split,
        When you, and those poor number saved with you,   10
        Hung on our driving boat, I saw your brother
        Most provident in peril, bind himself
        (Courage and hope both teaching him the practice)
        To a strong mast that lived upon the sea;
        Where like Arion on the dolphin's back   15
        I saw him hold acquaintance with the waves
        So long as I could see.
VIOLA For saying so, there's gold.
        Mine own escape unfoldeth to my hope,
        Whereto thy speech serves for authority,   20
        The like of him. Know'st thou this country?
CAPTAIN Ay, madam, well, for I was bred and born
        Not three hours' travel from this very place.
VIOLA Who governs here?
CAPTAIN A noble duke in nature as in name.   25
VIOLA What is his name?
CAPTAIN Orsino.
VIOLA Orsino! I have heard my father name him.
        He was a bachelor then.
CAPTAIN And so is now, or was so very late;   30
        For but a month ago I went from hence,
        And then 'twas fresh in murmur (as you know
        What great ones do, the less will prattle of)
        That he did seek the love of fair Olivia.
VIOLA What's she?   35
CAPTAIN A virtuous maid, the daughter of a count
        That died some twelvemonth since, then leaving her
        In the protection of his son, her brother,
        Who shortly also died; for whose dear love
        (They say) she hath abjured the sight   40
        And company of men.
VIOLA   O that I served that lady,
        And might not be delivered to the world
        Till I had made mine own occasion mellow
        What my estate is!
CAPTAIN   That were hard to compass,
        Because she will admit no kind of suit,   45
        No, not the duke's.

7

Viola says that she trusts the Captain. She plans to disguise herself as a man and become an attendant to Orsino. In Scene 3, Sir Toby Belch complains that Olivia's mourning prevents all enjoyment.

1 Appearance and reality (in groups of five or six)

In lines 48–9, Viola states one of Shakespeare's favourite themes: you can't judge by appearances. A beautiful appearance may conceal corruption ('nature with a beauteous wall/Doth oft close in pollution'). Much of *Twelfth Night* is about mistaken identity. Work out a tableau (a frozen picture) to illustrate Viola's comment. Each group shows its version to the class, 'freezing' the tableau for thirty seconds. Talk together about the similarities and differences in the various tableaux.

This 1955 production made Viola's first appearance strikingly dramatic. How would you stage Viola's entry? Think about how she would be dressed, and whether or not you would want to emphasise her high social status.

Conceal me what I am disguise my true identity	**allow** prove
haply appropriately	**hap** happen
The form of my intent my purpose	**mute** dumb servant
eunuch castrated male servant with a high-pitched voice	**By my troth** in faith
	cousin close relative (in Elizabethan times 'cousin' was loosely used)

VIOLA There is a fair behaviour in thee, captain,
 And though that nature with a beauteous wall
 Doth oft close in pollution, yet of thee
 I well believe thou hast a mind that suits 50
 With this thy fair and outward character.
 I prithee (and I'll pay thee bounteously)
 Conceal me what I am, and be my aid
 For such disguise as haply shall become
 The form of my intent. I'll serve this duke. 55
 Thou shalt present me as an eunuch to him –
 It may be worth thy pains – for I can sing,
 And speak to him in many sorts of music
 That will allow me very worth his service.
 What else may hap, to time I will commit, 60
 Only shape thou thy silence to my wit.
CAPTAIN Be you his eunuch, and your mute I'll be;
 When my tongue blabs, then let mine eyes not see.
VIOLA I thank thee. Lead me on.

Exeunt

ACT 1   SCENE 3
A room in Olivia's house

Enter SIR TOBY BELCH and MARIA

SIR TOBY What a plague means my niece to take the death of her
 brother thus? I am sure care's an enemy to life.
MARIA By my troth, Sir Toby, you must come in earlier o'nights. Your
 cousin, my lady, takes great exceptions to your ill hours.
SIR TOBY Why, let her except, before excepted. 5
MARIA Ay, but you must confine yourself within the modest limits of
 order.
SIR TOBY Confine? I'll confine myself no finer than I am: these clothes
 are good enough to drink in, and so be these boots too; and they
 be not, let them hang themselves in their own straps. 10

9

Maria warns Sir Toby that his drunkenness will be his downfall. She is scornful of Sir Andrew Aguecheek, thinking him stupid. Sir Andrew enters and immediately displays his foolishness.

1 Saying one thing, meaning another (in pairs)

Twelfth Night is rich in word-play. Sir Toby is a great juggler with words, even when he's been drinking. His description of Sir Andrew is full of mockery – he says one thing but means something else. Sir Toby calls Sir Andrew 'tall' (courageous), when he probably thinks him cowardly. Other descriptions would have had double meanings for Elizabethan audiences:

viol-de-gamboys a sexual joke: the viola da gamba is held between the knees

without book implies Andrew learnt by heart without understanding

nature picked up by Maria and turned into 'natural' (idiot)

Read Sir Toby's lines 16–23 aloud to each other. Speak them so that they sound like genuine praise. Then experiment with ways of saying them to show that you think Sir Andrew is really a fool and a coward.

2 *Castiliano vulgo*

No one is quite sure what Sir Toby's Spanish means (line 34). It could mean 'Look solemn' (like a Castilian from Spain), or 'Think of all Sir Andrew's money', or 'Talk of the devil', or perhaps 'More Spanish wine!'

Which meaning do you think is most in character with Sir Toby?

3 'A foolish knight' (in groups of three)

Sir Toby has invited Sir Andrew to Illyria to woo Olivia. Talk together about how you would present Sir Andrew on stage.

---

quaffing drunkenness
ducats gold coins
prodigal wastrel, spendthrift
viol-de-gamboys bass viol or viola de gamba
gust appetite, relish
substractors slanderers

coistrill worthless fellow, knave
parish top whipping top
shrew small mouse
Accost greet courteously
chambermaid lady companion, gentlewoman

MARIA That quaffing and drinking will undo you: I heard my lady talk
of it yesterday and of a foolish knight that you brought in one night
here to be her wooer.

SIR TOBY Who, Sir Andrew Aguecheek?

MARIA Ay, he.   15

SIR TOBY He's as tall a man as any's in Illyria.

MARIA What's that to th'purpose?

SIR TOBY Why, he has three thousand ducats a year.

MARIA Ay, but he'll have but a year in all these ducats. He's a very fool
and a prodigal.   20

SIR TOBY Fie, that you'll say so! He plays o'th'viol-de-gamboys, and
speaks three or four languages word for word without book, and
hath all the good gifts of nature.

MARIA He hath indeed all, most natural: for besides that he's a fool,
he's a great quarreller; and but that he hath the gift of a coward   25
to allay the gust he hath in quarrelling, 'tis thought among the
prudent he would quickly have the gift of a grave.

SIR TOBY By this hand, they are scoundrels and substractors that say
so of him. Who are they?

MARIA They that add, moreover, he's drunk nightly in your company.   30

SIR TOBY With drinking healths to my niece! I'll drink to her as long
as there is a passage in my throat and drink in Illyria; he's a coward
and a coistrill that will not drink to my niece till his brains turn
o'th'toe like a parish top. What, wench! *Castiliano vulgo*: for here
comes Sir Andrew Agueface.   35

Enter SIR ANDREW [AGUECHEEK]

SIR ANDREW Sir Toby Belch! How now, Sir Toby Belch?

SIR TOBY Sweet Sir Andrew!

SIR ANDREW Bless you, fair shrew.

MARIA And you too, sir.

SIR TOBY Accost, Sir Andrew, accost.   40

SIR ANDREW What's that?

SIR TOBY My niece's chambermaid.

SIR ANDREW Good Mistress Accost, I desire better acquaintance.

MARIA My name is Mary, sir.

SIR ANDREW Good Mistress Mary Accost –   45

SIR TOBY You mistake, knight. 'Accost' is front her, board her, woo
her, assail her.

SIR ANDREW By my troth, I would not undertake her in this company.
Is that the meaning of 'accost'?

Maria mocks Sir Andrew, then leaves. Sir Andrew tells Sir Toby that he intends to go home tomorrow because he is making no progress at all with his wooing of Olivia.

1 Stage business

Actors often invent actions ('business') to accompany lines 55–60. In one production, Maria took Sir Andrew's hand and placed it on the buttery-bar (a ledge for beer tankards). In another, to Sir Andrew's great embarrassment, she held his hand to her breast. Invent your own 'business' for these lines, remembering that 'dry' can also mean 'stupid', or 'thirsty', or 'sexually impotent'.

Sir Andrew and Sir Toby, Royal Shakespeare Company, 1974. In another production, Sir Andrew was played as surly, self-assured and aggressive, rather than merely foolish. Experiment to see how well that view of him would work by reading his lines aloud in a confident, angry and blustering manner. Decide whether it suits your impression of Sir Andrew.

And thou let part so if you let her go
barren empty of falseness
canary sweet wine (from the Canary Islands)
Christian . . . man average man
great eater of beef (see page 162)
Pourquoi why?

tongues languages
flax on a distaff (see page 162)
huswife hussy, prostitute (Elizabethans believed that sexually transmitted diseases caused loss of hair)
hard by nearby

MARIA Fare you well, gentlemen. [*Leaving*]   50

SIR TOBY And thou let part so, Sir Andrew, would thou mightst never
   draw sword again.

SIR ANDREW And you part so, mistress, I would I might never draw
   sword again. Fair lady, do you think you have fools in hand?

MARIA Sir, I have not you by th'hand.   55

SIR ANDREW Marry, but you shall have, and here's my hand.

MARIA Now, sir, thought is free. I pray you bring your hand to
   th'buttery-bar and let it drink.

SIR ANDREW Wherefore, sweetheart? What's your metaphor?

MARIA It's dry, sir.   60

SIR ANDREW Why, I think so: I am not such an ass but I can keep
   my hand dry. But what's your jest?

MARIA A dry jest, sir.

SIR ANDREW Are you full of them?

MARIA Ay, sir, I have them at my fingers' ends; marry, now I let go   65
   your hand, I am barren.   *Exit*

SIR TOBY O knight, thou lack'st a cup of canary. [*Hands him a cup*] When
   did I see thee so put down?

SIR ANDREW Never in your life, I think, unless you see canary put me
   down. Methinks sometimes I have no more wit than a Christian   70
   or an ordinary man has, but I am a great eater of beef, and I believe
   that does harm to my wit.

SIR TOBY No question.

SIR ANDREW And I thought that, I'd forswear it. I'll ride home
   tomorrow, Sir Toby.   75

SIR TOBY *Pourquoi*, my dear knight?

SIR ANDREW What is '*pourquoi*'? Do, or not do? I would I had
   bestowed that time in the tongues that I have in fencing, dancing,
   and bear-baiting. O had I but followed the arts!

SIR TOBY Then hadst thou had an excellent head of hair.   80

SIR ANDREW Why, would that have mended my hair?

SIR TOBY Past question, for thou seest it will not curl by nature.

SIR ANDREW But it becomes me well enough, does't not?

SIR TOBY Excellent; it hangs like flax on a distaff; and I hope to see
   a huswife take thee between her legs and spin it off.   85

SIR ANDREW Faith, I'll home tomorrow, Sir Toby; your niece will not
   be seen, or if she be, it's four to one, she'll none of me. The count
   himself here hard by woos her.

Sir Toby quickly persuades Sir Andrew to stay. Sir Andrew boasts about his dancing skills, and Sir Toby encourages him to perform.

1 Sir Toby the cunning persuader

In only three lines (lines 89–91), Sir Toby cunningly persuades Sir Andrew to stay in Illyria. Just how does he do it? Experiment with ways of speaking the lines, making each word or phrase as persuasive as possible. You have to make Sir Andrew believe that he really does have a strong chance of marrying Olivia.

2 Cutting a caper (in pairs)

Sir Toby encourages Sir Andrew to dance, naming popular dances of the day ('galliard' = a lively dance in triple time; 'coranto' = a rapid, running dance; 'jig' = a jerky, bouncy dance; 'sink-a-pace' = a dance with five steps; and notice that Sir Toby can't resist a rude joke: 'make water' = to urinate).

Take turns to say lines 102–8 to each other, demonstrating each dance. Remember, your intention is to get Sir Andrew to leap about, so make sure he can't resist your powerful invitation!

3 Unknowns: opportunities for invention

- No one knows for sure what 'the back-trick' is. Invent it.
- 'Mistress Mall' might be Maria in the play, or an attendant on Queen Elizabeth I, or an Elizabethan female thief. Imagine you have been invited to give a learned lecture to a conference of Shakespeare scholars and historians on 'Mistress Mall's picture'. Make it all up!

---

match marry
degree rank
estate fortune, wealth
there's life in't while there's life, there's hope
masques and revels theatricals (with masks) and dances
kickshawses trifles (from the French words *quelque chose* meaning 'something')

cut a caper leap (or spice for mutton)
mutton meat (or prostitute)
dun-coloured stock mouse-coloured stocking
Taurus the bull, a sign of the zodiac

SIR TOBY She'll none o'th'count; she'll not match above her degree, neither in estate, years, nor wit. I have heard her swear't. Tut, there's life in't, man.   90

SIR ANDREW I'll stay a month longer. I am a fellow o'th'strangest mind i'th'world: I delight in masques and revels sometimes altogether.

SIR TOBY Art thou good at these kickshawses, knight?

SIR ANDREW As any man in Illyria, whatsoever he be, under the degree of my betters, and yet I will not compare with an old man.   95

SIR TOBY What is thy excellence in a galliard, knight?

SIR ANDREW Faith, I can cut a caper.

SIR TOBY And I can cut the mutton to't.

SIR ANDREW And I think I have the back-trick simply as strong as any man in Illyria.   100

SIR TOBY Wherefore are these things hid? Wherefore have these gifts a curtain before 'em? Are they like to take dust, like Mistress Mall's picture? Why dost thou not go to church in a galliard and come home in a coranto? My very walk should be a jig; I would not so much as make water but in a sink-a-pace. What dost thou mean? Is it a world to hide virtues in? I did think, by the excellent constitution of thy leg, it was formed under the star of a galliard.   105

SIR ANDREW Ay, 'tis strong, and it does indifferent well in a dun-coloured stock. Shall we set about some revels?   110

SIR TOBY What shall we do else? Were we not born under Taurus?

SIR ANDREW Taurus? That's sides and heart.

SIR TOBY No, sir, it is legs and thighs. Let me see thee caper. Ha, higher; ha, ha, excellent!

Exeunt

Viola, disguised as Cesario, a page, has won the favour of Orsino. He has told her all his secrets. Now Orsino instructs Viola-Cesario to visit Olivia on his behalf to tell her of the strength of his love.

1 The new man – a cuckoo in the nest? (in pairs)

What does Valentine think of Viola-Cesario? This new 'man' has only been at court for three days, but is already highly favoured by Orsino. Take parts and read lines 1–8, experimenting with different tones for Valentine: jealous, angry, superior, indifferent, mocking, friendly. . . . Which tone do you prefer, and why?

Afterwards, discuss Valentine's reactions when he and the others are ordered to 'Stand you awhile aloof'.

2 A job interview (in groups of three)

How did Viola gain the post as page to Orsino? Improvise the missing scene in which the Captain presents her (as Cesario) to Orsino. The Duke will question them closely about their past, so Viola-Cesario and the Captain must have convincing stories!

3 Orsino's language (in pairs)

Shakespeare gives Orsino a distinctive way of speaking. For example, he says 'address thy gait unto her', a rather elaborate way of telling Viola-Cesario to visit Olivia. Try to express something of Orsino's style by taking parts and reading lines 9–41 to each other, but with Orsino deliberately exaggerating all the words and phrases which you think sound affected and self-important.

Change roles and repeat the activity. Then talk together about how you would describe Orsino's language, and whether or not you think it reflects his character.

---

much advanced promoted
humour moodiness, changeability
aloof apart
gait steps
leap all civil bounds don't stand
  on ceremony, be impolite

discourse story
nuncio's messenger's
grave aspect serious appearance

ACT 1   SCENE 4
Orsino's palace

Enter VALENTINE, *and* VIOLA in man's attire

VALENTINE If the duke continue these favours towards you, Cesario,
you are like to be much advanced; he hath known you but three
days, and already you are no stranger.

VIOLA You either fear his humour, or my negligence, that you call in
question the continuance of his love. Is he inconstant, sir, in his 5
favours?

VALENTINE No, believe me.

VIOLA I thank you. Here comes the count.

Enter DUKE [ORSINO], CURIO, *and Attendants*

ORSINO Who saw Cesario, ho?

VIOLA On your attendance, my lord, here. 10

ORSINO [*To Curio and Attendants*] Stand you awhile aloof. Cesario,
    Thou know'st no less but all: I have unclasped
    To thee the book even of my secret soul.
    Therefore, good youth, address thy gait unto her,
    Be not denied access; stand at her doors, 15
    And tell them there thy fixèd foot shall grow
    Till thou have audience.

VIOLA   Sure, my noble lord,
    If she be so abandoned to her sorrow
    As it is spoke, she never will admit me.

ORSINO Be clamorous, and leap all civil bounds, 20
    Rather than make unprofited return.

VIOLA Say I do speak with her, my lord, what then?

ORSINO O then unfold the passion of my love,
    Surprise her with discourse of my dear faith;
    It shall become thee well to act my woes: 25
    She will attend it better in thy youth
    Than in a nuncio's of more grave aspect.

Orsino praises the disguised Viola's feminine appearance. Viola reveals (in an aside) that she loves Orsino. In Scene 5, Feste won't take Maria seriously when she tells him he's in trouble.

1 Dramatic irony

Scene 4 is rich in dramatic irony (where the audience knows something that a character on stage does not know). Orsino does not know that he is speaking to a female when he praises Cesario, saying how like a woman 'he' looks. For Shakespeare's audience there was a heightened level of irony, because at that time only males were allowed to act. So Viola-Cesario was a boy, playing a girl, playing a boy!

How do you think Viola-Cesario would react to lines 28–33? One person reads, the other tries out various reactions (for example, should she wink at the audience, or would that be out of character?).

2 What *does* she see in him? (in small groups)

Viola has fallen in love with Orsino (line 41). It looks like love at first sight. Talk together about what you think Viola sees in Orsino to make her love him.

3 Word-play: beware of over-explanation!

Feste begins Scene 5 with a pun: dead men see no colours (collars or hangmen's nooses), so they don't fear them. The Elizabethans enjoyed such punning jokes, in which the way in which a word was pronounced could give it different meanings (see page 164). Puns are still popular today, but not all of the word-play humour in *Twelfth Night* is immediately obvious to a modern audience or reader. The following pages give you help to understand and enjoy the humour, without killing it stone dead.

---

belie mistake
Diana the moon goddess
  (associated with love)
rubious ruby-red
pipe voice
is semblative resembles

constellation destiny foretold by
  the stars (see page 35)
barful obstacle-filled
Make that good prove it
good lenten answer weak joke
  (like a simple meal in Lent)

VIOLA I think not so, my lord.

ORSINO   Dear lad, believe it;
    For they shall yet belie thy happy years
    That say thou art a man: Diana's lip   30
    Is not more smooth and rubious; thy small pipe
    Is as the maiden's organ, shrill and sound,
    And all is semblative a woman's part.
    I know thy constellation is right apt
    For this affair. Some four or five attend him –   35
    All if you will, for I myself am best
    When least in company. Prosper well in this,
    And thou shalt live as freely as thy lord
    To call his fortunes thine.

VIOLA   I'll do my best
    To woo your lady. [*Aside*] Yet a barful strife!   40
    Whoe'er I woo, myself would be his wife.

                                     Exeunt

ACT 1   SCENE 5
Olivia's house

Enter MARIA and FESTE

MARIA Nay, either tell me where thou hast been, or I will not open my
    lips so wide as a bristle may enter in way of thy excuse. My lady
    will hang thee for thy absence.

FESTE Let her hang me: he that is well hanged in this world needs to
    fear no colours.   5

MARIA Make that good.

FESTE He shall see none to fear.

MARIA A good lenten answer. I can tell thee where that saying was born,
    of 'I fear no colours.'

FESTE Where, good Mistress Mary?   10

MARIA In the wars, and that may you be bold to say in your foolery.

FESTE Well, God give them wisdom that have it; and those that are
    fools, let them use their talents.

Feste continues to joke with Maria. He hints at her relationship with Sir Toby. Olivia orders Feste to leave, but he challenges her by offering to prove she is a fool.

1 Repartee (in pairs)

Maria and Feste are like a comedy duo, scoring points off each other in quick-fire exchanges (repartee). Take parts and read lines 1–26 as a pair of vaudeville comics in a music-hall or on television. Add gestures and expressions to add to the humour.

2 'This simple syllogism'

A syllogism is a logical argument which moves carefully from one point to the next. Feste mocks this philosophical method of reasoning in lines 35–43, but, as usual, there is some sense in what he says. Imagine the actor playing Feste says to you: 'Look, I want to play these lines like a philosophy teacher proving an argument. How can I go about it? What gestures and props can I use?' Advise him!

3 The Fool

Don't think that because Feste is called the Fool, he is foolish. He is always playing with words, and occasionally seems to talk nonsense (like inventing an imaginary philosopher, Quinapalus). But there's often a lot of truth in what he says. Feste reminds Olivia that he has all his wits about him: 'I wear not motley in my brain'. His Latin quotation *'cucullus non facit monachum'* (the hood does not make the monk) is yet another reminder of a major theme of the play: don't judge by outward appearances.

As you read on, keep thinking about what kind of Fool Feste is. You'll find he's a very complex character.

---

to be turned away dismissed, sacked
points matters or laces (a pun)
gaskins wide breeches held up with laces ('points')
Eve's flesh womanhood
madonna my lady

botcher mender of old clothes
syllogism argument
cuckold deceived husband
Misprision error
motley Fool's clothes (see page 70)
Dexteriously skilfully

MARIA Yet you will be hanged for being so long absent – or to be turned
    away: is not that as good as a hanging to you?   15
FESTE Many a good hanging prevents a bad marriage; and for turning
    away, let summer bear it out.
MARIA You are resolute then?
FESTE Not so neither, but I am resolved on two points –
MARIA That if one break, the other will hold, or if both break, your   20
    gaskins fall.
FESTE Apt, in good faith, very apt. Well, go thy way; if Sir Toby would
    leave drinking, thou wert as witty a piece of Eve's flesh as any in
    Illyria.
MARIA Peace, you rogue, no more o'that; here comes my lady: make   25
    your excuse wisely, you were best.   [*Exit*]

      Enter LADY OLIVIA [*attended,*] *with* MALVOLIO

FESTE Wit, and't be thy will, put me into good fooling! Those wits that
    think they have thee do very oft prove fools, and I that am sure I
    lack thee may pass for a wise man. For what says Quinapalus?
    'Better a witty fool than a foolish wit' – God bless thee, lady.   30
OLIVIA Take the fool away.
FESTE Do you not hear, fellows? Take away the lady.
OLIVIA Go to, y'are a dry fool: I'll no more of you; besides, you grow
    dishonest.
FESTE Two faults, madonna, that drink and good counsel will amend: 35
    for give the dry fool drink, then is the fool not dry; bid the dishonest
    man mend himself; if he mend, he is no longer dishonest; if he
    cannot, let the botcher mend him. Anything that's mended is but
    patched: virtue that transgresses is but patched with sin, and sin
    that amends is but patched with virtue. If that this simple syllogism   40
    will serve, so; if it will not, what remedy? As there is no true cuckold
    but calamity, so beauty's a flower. The lady bade take away the fool;
    therefore I say again, take her away.
OLIVIA Sir, I bade them take away you.
FESTE Misprision in the highest degree! Lady, *cucullus non facit*   45
    monachum: that's as much to say as I wear not motley in my brain.
    Good madonna, give me leave to prove you a fool.
OLIVIA Can you do it?
FESTE Dexteriously, good madonna.
OLIVIA Make your proof.   50

Feste 'proves' Olivia to be a fool, but is treated with contempt by Malvolio. Olivia criticises Malvolio's sour attitude, urging greater charity and generosity of spirit. Maria tells of a visitor.

Malvolio, Royal Shakespeare Company, 1983.

1 Malvolio's tone of voice?

Pinch your nose between forefinger and thumb, lean your head back, and speak Malvolio's lines slowly, pausing after every punctuation mark. Listen to the note of superiority, condescension and disdain in your voice. Is that how you think Malvolio speaks?

Malvolio doesn't criticise only Feste, he also patronises Olivia. The first and last sentences in lines 67–72 are barbed criticisms of Olivia and her dead father. Experiment with different ways of saying the lines, for example: sneeringly, pompously, seriously, laughingly.

---

catechise question
bide await
mend get better (but Malvolio interprets it as 'get worse')
no fox not cunning
crow laugh uproariously
zanies foolish assistants
distempered unwholesome

bird-bolts blunt arrows
allowed licensed, free to speak his mind (see page 170)
rail reproach, mock
Mercury god of deceit
endue thee with leasing teach you to lie

FESTE I must catechise you for it, madonna. Good my mouse of virtue, answer me.

OLIVIA Well, sir, for want of other idleness, I'll bide your proof.

FESTE Good madonna, why mourn'st thou?

OLIVIA Good fool, for my brother's death   55

FESTE I think his soul is in hell, madonna.

OLIVIA I know his soul is in heaven, fool.

FESTE The more fool, madonna, to mourn for your brother's soul being in heaven. Take away the fool, gentlemen.

OLIVIA What think you of this fool, Malvolio? Doth he not mend?   60

MALVOLIO Yes, and shall do, till the pangs of death shake him; infirmity, that decays the wise, doth ever make the better fool.

FESTE God send you, sir, a speedy infirmity, for the better increasing your folly! Sir Toby will be sworn that I am no fox, but he will not pass his word for twopence that you are no fool.   65

OLIVIA How say you to that, Malvolio?

MALVOLIO I marvel your ladyship takes delight in such a barren rascal. I saw him put down the other day with an ordinary fool that has no more brain than a stone. Look you now, he's out of his guard already. Unless you laugh and minister occasion to him, he is   70
gagged. I protest I take these wise men that crow so at these set kind of fools no better than the fools' zanies.

OLIVIA O you are sick of self-love, Malvolio, and taste with a distempered appetite. To be generous, guiltless, and of free disposition is to take those things for bird-bolts that you deem   75
cannon bullets. There is no slander in an allowed fool though he do nothing but rail; nor no railing in a known discreet man though he do nothing but reprove.

FESTE Now Mercury endue thee with leasing, for thou speak'st well of fools!   80

Enter MARIA

MARIA Madam, there is at the gate a young gentleman much desires to speak with you.

OLIVIA From the Count Orsino, is it?

MARIA I know not, madam; 'tis a fair young man and well attended.

OLIVIA Who of my people hold him in delay?   85

MARIA Sir Toby, madam, your kinsman.

Olivia sends Malvolio to dismiss the visitor. Sir Toby, who is drunk, muddles his words. Malvolio returns to explain that the visitor insists on speaking to Olivia.

1 Playing a drunk (in groups of three)

It's very difficult to play the part of a drunken man convincingly. Can you do it? Take turns to play Sir Toby, Feste and Olivia, and act out lines 96–106. Two actors' tips for imitating a drunk:

'Imagine your left foot is nailed to the floor. Try to walk in all directions with the other.'

'Drunks have problems with speaking and hearing. They misunderstand, like Sir Toby who confuses 'lethargy' and 'lechery'. Struggle with your words, but remember you have to make them perfectly clear to the audience, even if you slur them. So, take your time and search slowly for each word in your mind, as if you are having difficulty finding them.'

2 It's a comedy! (in small groups)

Twice in the lines opposite Shakespeare may be reminding you not to take *Twelfth Night* too seriously, but just to enjoy it as a comedy.

- Line 90 contains the subtitle of the play: 'what you will' (whatever you like). The saying was in common use in Shakespeare's time.
- Sir Toby's line 106 ('Well, it's all one') is the Elizabethan equivalent of 'So what?', or 'I couldn't care less'. The expression is used several times in the play. It echoes the subtitle of the play.

One person takes the role of William Shakespeare. The others tell 'Shakespeare' that *Twelfth Night* is now studied for examinations, and that scholarly books are written on it. What does he reply?

---

suit message of love
old stale, not funny
Jove king of the gods (see page 165)
pia mater brain
sot drunk
lethargy sleepiness

one draught above heat the first warm drink
crowner coroner
sit o'my coz hold an inquest on my cousin
look to look after

OLIVIA Fetch him off, I pray you; he speaks nothing but madman. Fie
on him.

[Exit Maria]

Go you, Malvolio. If it be a suit from the count, I am sick, or not
at home – what you will to dismiss it.   90

Exit Malvolio

Now you see, sir, how your fooling grows old, and people dislike
it.

FESTE Thou hast spoke for us, madonna, as if thy eldest son should be
a fool: whose skull Jove cram with brains, for – here he comes –

Enter SIR TOBY *[staggering]*

one of thy kin has a most weak *pia mater*.   95

OLIVIA By mine honour, half drunk! What is he at the gate, cousin?

SIR TOBY A gentleman.

OLIVIA A gentleman? What gentleman?

SIR TOBY 'Tis a gentleman here – *[Hiccuping]* a plague o'these pickle
herring! How now, sot?   100

FESTE Good Sir Toby –

OLIVIA Cousin, cousin, how have you come so early by this lethargy?

SIR TOBY Lechery! I defy lechery. There's one at the gate.

OLIVIA Ay, marry, what is he?

SIR TOBY Let him be the devil and he will, I care not: give me faith,   105
say I. Well, it's all one.   *Exit*

OLIVIA What's a drunken man like, fool?

FESTE Like a drowned man, a fool, and a madman: one draught above
heat makes him a fool, the second mads him, and a third drowns
him.   110

OLIVIA Go thou and seek the crowner, and let him sit o'my coz, for
he's in the third degree of drink: he's drowned. Go look after him.

FESTE He is but mad yet, madonna, and the fool shall look to the
madman.   *[Exit]*

Enter MALVOLIO

MALVOLIO Madam, yond young fellow swears he will speak with you.   115
I told him you were sick; he takes on him to understand so much
and therefore comes to speak with you. I told him you were asleep;
he seems to have a foreknowledge of that too, and therefore comes
to speak with you. What is to be said to him, lady? He's fortified
against any denial.   120

Malvolio haughtily describes Viola's appearance. Olivia commands Maria to veil her. Viola enters (disguised as Cesario) and seeks to discover which woman is Olivia.

1 Betwixt and between (in small groups)

Malvolio's description of Viola-Cesario (lines 130–4) is full of comparisons: like an unripe apple ('codling/apple'); like the time when the tide turns ('in standing water').

What's your idea of Viola-Cesario's appearance? Collect illustrations from newspapers and magazines of individuals who you think match Malvolio's description.

2 Viola-Cesario's high-flown speech of love

Viola-Cesario begins her address to Olivia in high style: 'Most radiant, exquisite, and unmatchable beauty'. But she is disconcerted by not knowing if it is really Olivia she is speaking to. She never gets to finish the elaborate speech she has so carefully prepared, or which Orsino may well have written for her. Write the next few lines of her prepared speech to follow on from her high-sounding opening words.

3 Acting a part

Notice the way Shakespeare includes references to the theatre: 'speech', 'well penned', 'con' (learn by heart), 'studied', 'part', 'comedian' (actor), 'play'. You will find other mentions of acting as you read on.

Viola says 'I am not that I play' (line 153). What advice (on expression, gesture or tone) would you give to the actor playing Viola to help her make the audience laugh at this line?

---

sheriff's post post outside a sheriff's door (for notices)
supporter to a bench prop
squash unripe peapod
peascod peapod
codling unripe apple
shrewishly sharply

cast away waste
comptible sensitive
least sinister usage slightest discourtesy
comedian actor
usurp betray

OLIVIA Tell him he shall not speak with me.

MALVOLIO H'as been told so; and he says he'll stand at your door like a sheriff's post, and be the supporter to a bench, but he'll speak with you.

OLIVIA What kind o'man is he?   125

MALVOLIO Why, of mankind.

OLIVIA What manner of man?

MALVOLIO Of very ill manner: he'll speak with you, will you or no.

OLIVIA Of what personage and years is he?

MALVOLIO Not yet old enough for a man, nor young enough for a boy: 130
as a squash is before 'tis a peascod, or a codling when 'tis almost an apple. 'Tis with him in standing water, between boy and man. He is very well-favoured and he speaks very shrewishly. One would think his mother's milk were scarce out of him.

OLIVIA Let him approach. Call in my gentlewoman.   135

MALVOLIO Gentlewoman, my lady calls.   *Exit*

Enter MARIA

OLIVIA Give me my veil; come throw it o'er my face.
We'll once more hear Orsino's embassy.

Enter VIOLA

VIOLA The honourable lady of the house, which is she?

OLIVIA Speak to me; I shall answer for her. Your will?   140

VIOLA Most radiant, exquisite, and unmatchable beauty – I pray you tell me if this be the lady of the house, for I never saw her. I would be loath to cast away my speech: for besides that it is excellently well penned, I have taken great pains to con it. Good beauties, let me sustain no scorn; I am very comptible, even to the least sinister   145
usage.

OLIVIA Whence came you, sir?

VIOLA I can say little more than I have studied, and that question's out of my part. Good gentle one, give me modest assurance if you be the lady of the house, that I may proceed in my speech.   150

OLIVIA Are you a comedian?

VIOLA No, my profound heart; and yet, by the very fangs of malice, I swear, I am not that I play. Are you the lady of the house?

OLIVIA If I do not usurp myself, I am.

After some verbal fencing, Viola says her message is for Olivia alone.
Maria is dismissed. Olivia questions Viola, who asks to see her face.
Olivia unveils.

1 Helping the audience

Shakespeare's audience would have been more familiar with certain expressions than we are today (see page 162). Suggest how an actor could help a modern audience to understand the following phrases:

lines 164–5 ''Tis not that time of moon with me to make one in so skipping a dialogue' (the moon was thought to bring on lunacy).

line 173 'taxation of homage' (a demand for submission and loyalty).

line 180 'What is your text?' (Olivia begins a catechism, questioning Viola in a similar form to the questions and responses used in church).

line 186 'To answer by the method' (to make the reply in the appropriate style in this catechism you are putting me through).

lines 191–2 'such a one I was this present' (this is a recent portrait of me).

2 Olivia's unveiling (in small groups)

Olivia has vowed to mourn her dead brother and to avoid men for seven years. Yet she has begun to respond in a very positive way to Viola-Cesario's liveliness. At line 191 she unveils her face. This is a very significant gesture, which suggests that her thoughts and feelings are very far from being sad ones. Olivia has evidently become fascinated by the appearance and language of Viola-Cesario.

Talk together about just where in the script you think Olivia begins to be attracted by Viola-Cesario. Work out how you would stage the encounter to show Olivia's growing fascination.

---

usurp wrong (by withholding from marriage)
from my commission not part of my instructions
feigned pretended
make one in join in
swabber deck-cleaner, sailor
hull float, stay

mollification calming down, appeasement
the olive olive branch of peace
entertainment reception
maidenhead virginity
by the method in the style
heresy false doctrine, contrary belief

VIOLA Most certain, if you are she, you do usurp yourself: for what is   155
yours to bestow is not yours to reserve. But this is from my
commission. I will on with my speech in your praise, and then show
you the heart of my message.

OLIVIA Come to what is important in't: I forgive you the praise.

VIOLA Alas, I took great pains to study it, and 'tis poetical.   160

OLIVIA It is the more like to be feigned; I pray you keep it in. I heard
you were saucy at my gates, and allowed your approach rather to
wonder at you than to hear you. If you be not mad, be gone; if
you have reason, be brief. 'Tis not that time of moon with me to
make one in so skipping a dialogue.   165

MARIA Will you hoist sail, sir? Here lies your way.

VIOLA No, good swabber, I am to hull here a little longer. Some
mollification for your giant, sweet lady! Tell me your mind, I am
a messenger.

OLIVIA Sure you have some hideous matter to deliver, when the   170
courtesy of it is so fearful. Speak your office.

VIOLA It alone concerns your ear. I bring no overture of war, no
taxation of homage; I hold the olive in my hand; my words are as
full of peace as matter.

OLIVIA Yet you began rudely. What are you? What would you?   175

VIOLA The rudeness that hath appeared in me I learned from my
entertainment. What I am, and what I would, are as secret as
maidenhead: to your ears, divinity; to any other's, profanation.

OLIVIA Give us the place alone; we will hear this divinity.
                              [*Exeunt Maria and Attendants*]
Now, sir, what is your text?   180

VIOLA Most sweet lady –

OLIVIA A comfortable doctrine, and much may be said of it. Where lies
your text?

VIOLA In Orsino's bosom.

OLIVIA In his bosom? In what chapter of his bosom?   185

VIOLA To answer by the method, in the first of his heart.

OLIVIA O I have read it. It is heresy. Have you no more to say?

VIOLA Good madam, let me see your face.

OLIVIA Have you any commission from your lord to negotiate with my
face? You are now out of your text, but we will draw the curtain   190
and show you the picture. [*Unveiling*] Look you, sir, such a one I
was this present. Is't not well done?

Viola accuses Olivia of keeping her beauty to herself by not having children. Olivia replies mockingly. Viola explains that if she were the one who loved Olivia, every action would express her love and move Olivia to pity her.

1 Mocking copy: prose and verse (in pairs)

In lines 197–9, Viola appeals to Olivia to marry and have children ('copy'). In this way, Olivia can ensure that her beauty is handed on and kept alive in the world after her death. Viola's plea echoes the theme of the first fourteen of Shakespeare's *Sonnets*. But Olivia mocks Viola by taking 'copy' literally. She proposes to leave various lists ('divers schedules') itemising all the elements of her beauty.

Talk together about why you think Shakespeare gives Olivia prose to reply to Viola's heightened poetry (see page 165).

2 Orsino's qualities (in groups of five to eight)

Olivia lists at least nine of Orsino's qualities in lines 213–17. Identify his various qualities, then prepare a series of tableaux (frozen pictures) to show each one (for example, 'virtuous', 'noble', and so on). Present your version to the class and compare it with other groups' presentations of 'Orsino's qualities'.

3 Famous lines (in small groups)

Lines 223–31 are some of Shakespeare's best-known love poetry. Work out how to present the lines in a dramatically effective way, such as through choral speaking, or by sharing out the lines, or by adding sound effects or mimes, or as a song, or by echoing particular words and phrases (the 'willow' was an emblem of sorrowful love; 'cantons' are songs; 'contemnèd' means rejected or despised; 'Hallow' means shout and 'babbling gossip' means echo).

---

in grain natural, indelible
blent blended
divers schedules various lists
inventoried classified
'praise value
Could be but recompensed would receive no more than its due reward

nonpareil incomparable, unequalled
In voices well divulged well spoken of, high reputation
flame passion
reverberate echoing

VIOLA Excellently done, if God did all.

OLIVIA 'Tis in grain, sir; 'twill endure wind and weather.

VIOLA 'Tis beauty truly blent, whose red and white   195
    Nature's own sweet and cunning hand laid on.
    Lady, you are the cruell'st she alive,
    If you will lead these graces to the grave,
    And leave the world no copy.

OLIVIA O sir, I will not be so hard-hearted: I will give out divers   200
schedules of my beauty. It shall be inventoried and every particle
and utensil labelled to my will, as, *item*, two lips, indifferent red;
item, two grey eyes, with lids to them; *item*, one neck, one chin,
and so forth. Were you sent hither to 'praise me?

VIOLA I see you what you are. You are too proud;   205
    But if you were the devil, you are fair!
    My lord and master loves you. O such love
    Could be but recompensed, though you were crowned
    The nonpareil of beauty.

OLIVIA   How does he love me?

VIOLA With adorations, fertile tears,   210
    With groans that thunder love, with sighs of fire.

OLIVIA Your lord does know my mind. I cannot love him.
    Yet I suppose him virtuous, know him noble,
    Of great estate, of fresh and stainless youth;
    In voices well divulged, free, learned, and valiant,   215
    And in dimension, and the shape of nature,
    A gracious person. But yet I cannot love him.
    He might have took his answer long ago.

VIOLA If I did love you in my master's flame,
    With such a suff'ring, such a deadly life,   220
    In your denial I would find no sense;
    I would not understand it.

OLIVIA   Why, what would you?

VIOLA Make me a willow cabin at your gate,
    And call upon my soul within the house;
    Write loyal cantons of contemnèd love,   225
    And sing them loud even in the dead of night;
    Hallow your name to the reverberate hills,
    And make the babbling gossip of the air
    Cry out 'Olivia!' O you should not rest
    Between the elements of air and earth   230
    But you should pity me!

Viola rejects payment. She leaves, wishing that Olivia, like Orsino, may suffer from rejected love. Olivia fears that she is falling in love with Viola-Cesario. She sends Malvolio on a false errand to ensure that Viola returns.

1 'You' and 'thou' (in pairs)

Elizabethans frequently used 'thou' or 'thy' to address someone who was especially close or loved. 'You' was a rather more distant way of talking to someone for whom you did not have special affection.

Read aloud everything Olivia says in lines 231–48. Emphasise strongly each 'you', 'your', 'thou' and 'thee'. Talk together about what you discover.

2 Judging by appearances?

Olivia judges Viola-Cesario to be a 'gentleman' by five qualities ('five-fold blazon', line 248): speech, looks, body, behaviour and spirit. But at line 264, Olivia fears that she may have been deceived by appearances: 'Mine eye too great a flatterer for my mind'. Certainly, she has been deceived by Viola-Cesario's outward appearance.

● Do you believe that you can judge someone's true quality by their appearance, whatever their current social status? Could you recognise a prince even if he were dressed in rags?

● Talk together about each of the five qualities (line 247) in turn to decide if you think they are a reliable guide to character.

3 'What is decreed must be'

Carry out a survey of your class to discover how many of you agree or disagree with Viola's claim (line 266) that Fate determines our love life. Talk together about whether or not you believe in Fate. (See also page 35.)

---

fortunes present social status
my state is well I'm content
fee'd post paid messenger
fervour passionate love
blazon coat of arms, marks of
  gentility

catch the plague fall in love
peevish irritating
county's Count Orsino's
owe own

OLIVIA   You might do much.
          What is your parentage?
VIOLA Above my fortunes, yet my state is well:
          I am a gentleman.
OLIVIA   Get you to your lord.
          I cannot love him Let him send no more –   235
          Unless (perchance) you come to me again,
          To tell me how he takes it. Fare you well.
          I thank you for your pains. Spend this for me.
VIOLA I am no fee'd post, lady; keep your purse;
          My master, not myself, lacks recompense.   240
          Love make his heart of flint that you shall love,
          And let your fervour like my master's be
          Placed in contempt. Farewell, fair cruelty.   *Exit*
OLIVIA 'What is your parentage?'
          'Above my fortunes, yet my state is well: 245
          I am a gentleman.' I'll be sworn thou art;
          Thy tongue, thy face, thy limbs, actions, and spirit
          Do give thee five-fold blazon. Not too fast! Soft, soft!
          Unless the master were the man – How now?
          Even so quickly may one catch the plague?   250
          Methinks I feel this youth's perfections
          With an invisible and subtle stealth
          To creep in at mine eyes. Well, let it be.
          What ho, Malvolio!

                         Enter MALVOLIO

MALVOLIO   Here, madam, at your service.
OLIVIA Run after that same peevish messenger,   255
          The county's man. He left this ring behind him,
          Would I, or not. Tell him, I'll none of it.
          Desire him not to flatter with his lord,
          Nor hold him up with hopes; I am not for him.
          If that the youth will come this way tomorrow,   260
          I'll give him reasons for't. Hie thee, Malvolio!
MALVOLIO Madam, I will.   *Exit*
OLIVIA I do I know not what, and fear to find
          Mine eye too great a flatterer for my mind.
          Fate, show thy force; ourselves we do not owe.   265
          What is decreed must be; and be this so.   *[Exit]*

Looking back at Act 1
Activities for groups or individuals

1 Five scenes, five headlines

There are five scenes in Act 1. Write five headlines to sum up the main action of each scene.

2 What is the play about?

Certain themes run all through the play: music, love, the sea, disguise, death and folly. Find two examples of each theme in Act 1.

3 Where is Illyria?

Historical Illyria lay along the Adriatic coast of present-day Albania and Croatia. But *Twelfth Night* is set in a never-never land of romantic comedy, where anything can happen. Imagine you are about to stage a production of the play. How will you present Illyria, the world of illusion? Will you give your production a Mediterranean atmosphere, a setting in Elizabethan England, or some other location? Look through the illustrations in this edition, then work out your own ideas for a set. Sketch several costumes to match your chosen setting.

4 Coats of arms

Design a coat of arms ('blazon') for Sir Toby. It should illustrate his belief that 'care's an enemy to life' (melancholy is an enemy to enjoyment – or, be happy!). Also design coats of arms for the other characters, including a suitable motto for each.

5 Viola-Cesario: young woman as young man

When Viola first appears as Cesario, do you think that the audience should immediately be able to recognise her? Make notes on what she wears and other ways in which she tries to resemble a young man.

6 On with the motley

The traditional costume for a Fool or clown was 'motley' (see page 70). But every production of *Twelfth Night* presents its own style of costume for Feste. How would he be dressed in your production?

7 Determined by the stars?

'Were we not born under Taurus?' says Sir Toby to Sir Andrew as they enjoy their revels. Taurus (the bull) is one of the twelve signs of the zodiac. People who believe in astrology think that a person's character and personality are influenced by the star signs they are born under (you'll find that Act 2 begins with a character who says just that). But do *you* believe it? Make a list of reasons to explain why you agree or disagree with Sir Toby's belief.

8 Love at first sight?

Love strikes like lightning in Act 1. Orsino fell in love with Olivia at first sight ('That instant was I turned into a hart'). Similarly, Viola has fallen in love with Orsino ('Whoe'er I woo, myself would be his wife'). Olivia asks herself 'Even so quickly may one catch the plague?'.

Do you believe in love at first sight? Talk together about whether or not you believe you can fall head over heels in love 'in an instant'.

'O then unfold the passion of my love.' Orsino and Viola. Compare this picture with the illustration on page 56.

*Antonio has rescued Sebastian from the shipwreck and wishes to be his
servant. Sebastian rejects Antonio's offer and tells of his grief for his twin
sister Viola, whom he believes drowned.*

1 Parallels (in pairs)

This scene has many echoes of Act 1 Scene 2. Take parts and read
through the whole scene. Then read through Act 1 Scene 2 and
identify the similarities by answering these questions:

a What kind of person rescued Viola and Sebastian?
b Where does each twin say they intend to go?
c Who wants to be the servant of each twin?
d Are there any other parallels between Sebastian's situation and
   Viola's?
e If you were directing the play, would you have Sebastian dressed
   identically to Viola? Give reasons for your decision.

2 Does Sebastian cry?

The actor playing Sebastian asks for your advice: 'Do lines 22–3
mean that I actually cry salt tears here?' What do you reply?

3 A puzzle

Many people find it puzzling that Sebastian and Antonio apologise to
each other in lines 24–5. Talk together about possible explanations
(there could be hints in what they have already said to each other).
Then consider how you could make sense of the lines for the
audience. Work out what the actors could do to suggest reasons for
their apologies to each other.

---

malignancy evil influence
distemper infect
sooth truly, indeed
determinate voyage plan for travel
mere extravagancy only
  wandering
in manners the rather in courtesy

breach surf, breaking waves
with such estimable wonder in
  all modesty
publish proclaim, describe
entertainment treatment,
  hospitality

ACT 2 SCENE 1
The sea-coast of Illyria

Enter ANTONIO *and* SEBASTIAN

ANTONIO Will you stay no longer? Nor will you not that I go with you?

SEBASTIAN By your patience, no. My stars shine darkly over me; the malignancy of my fate might perhaps distemper yours; therefore I shall crave of you your leave that I may bear my evils alone. It were a bad recompense for your love to lay any of them on you. 5

ANTONIO Let me know of you whither you are bound.

SEBASTIAN No, sooth, sir. My determinate voyage is mere extravagancy. But I perceive in you so excellent a touch of modesty that you will not extort from me what I am willing to keep in. Therefore it charges me in manners the rather to express myself. You must know 10 of me then, Antonio, my name is Sebastian (which I called Roderigo); my father was that Sebastian of Messaline whom I know you have heard of. He left behind him myself and a sister, both born in an hour: if the heavens had been pleased, would we had so ended! But you, sir, altered that, for some hour before you took 15 me from the breach of the sea was my sister drowned.

ANTONIO Alas the day!

SEBASTIAN A lady, sir, though it was said she much resembled me, was yet of many accounted beautiful; but though I could not with such estimable wonder overfar believe that, yet thus far I will boldly 20 publish her: she bore a mind that envy could not but call fair. She is drowned already, sir, with salt water, though I seem to drown her remembrance again with more.

ANTONIO Pardon me, sir, your bad entertainment.

SEBASTIAN O good Antonio, forgive me your trouble. 25

ANTONIO If you will not murder me for my love, let me be your servant.

Sebastian again rejects Antonio's offer of service, but Antonio determines to follow him, without fear. In Scene 2, Viola puzzles over Malvolio's message: has Olivia fallen in love with her?

1 'She took the ring of me' (in small groups)

Viola tells a downright lie to Malvolio in line 10. Why? Talk together about what it suggests to you about her character.

How does Malvolio return the ring? Invent a way for Malvolio to return the ring in a manner that suits his personality. In one production he slipped it over his long staff of office and let it slide slowly down to Viola's feet. Speak 'Receive it so' and lines 11–13 as you explore the various possibilities.

on a moderate pace without hurrying
desperate assurance hopeless certainty

hardy bold

SEBASTIAN If you will not undo what you have done, that is, kill him
whom you have recovered, desire it not. Fare ye well at once; my
bosom is full of kindness, and I am yet so near the manners of my
mother that, upon the least occasion more, mine eyes will tell tales   30
of me. I am bound to the Count Orsino's court. Farewell.   *Exit*
ANTONIO The gentleness of all the gods go with thee!
    I have many enemies in Orsino's court,
    Else would I very shortly see thee there.
    But come what may, I do adore thee so   35
    That danger shall seem sport, and I will go.   *Exit*

ACT 2   SCENE 2
A street near Olivia's house

Enter VIOLA and MALVOLIO

MALVOLIO Were you not even now with the Countess Olivia?
VIOLA Even now, sir; on a moderate pace, I have since arrived but
hither.
MALVOLIO She returns this ring to you. You might have saved me my
pains to have taken it away yourself. She adds, moreover, that you   5
should put your lord into a desperate assurance: she will none of
him. And one thing more, that you be never so hardy to come again
in his affairs, unless it be to report your lord's taking of this. Receive
it so.
VIOLA She took the ring of me. I'll none of it.   10
MALVOLIO Come, sir, you peevishly threw it to her; and her will is,
it should be so returned. If it be worth stooping for, there it lies,
in your eye; if not, be it his that finds it.   *Exit*
VIOLA I left no ring with her: what means this lady?
    Fortune forbid my outside have not charmed her!   15
    She made good view of me, indeed so much
    That, methought, her eyes had lost her tongue,
    For she did speak in starts distractedly.

Perplexed, Viola fears Olivia loves her, whilst she herself loves Orsino. She hopes that time will resolve the difficulties. Scene 3 finds Sir Toby and Sir Andrew have been drinking all night.

1 Viola's soliloquy

Viola realises (lines 14–38) that her disguise as a man has caused Olivia to fall in love with her. Explore her soliloquy in one or more of the following ways:

a Learn the lines by heart and act them out to the class as if you were auditioning for a place at drama school.

b The soliloquy is rather like a conversation. Viola asks herself questions and tries to answer them. In pairs, try it as a telephone conversation. Each partner reads a sentence (or up to a semi-colon) and the other partner replies with the next sentence (or 'sense unit').

c Walk around the room reading the lines aloud. At every new thought, change direction.

d Take parts as Viola, Olivia, Malvolio and Orsino. One person reads slowly. As any character is mentioned, everyone points at him or her: '"I" *(all point to Viola)* left no ring with "her" *(all point to Olivia)*', and so on.

e Add gestures and facial expressions to illustrate each section.

2 Drunk again! (in pairs)

To get yourself in the mood for Scene 3, take parts and read lines 1–12 in the style of drunken men. Say the lines very, very slowly as if you were befuddled, but trying to develop a logical argument. Remember: it's late, and they've been drinking heavily . . .

---

churlish rude
pregnant enemy crafty fiend, the devil, Satan
proper-false handsome deceivers
waxen easily moulded, changeable
fadge turn out, develop
dote on be infatuated with

thriftless unprofitable, wasted
betimes early
diluculo surgere rising at dawn is healthy (a Latin saying)
by my troth truly
can tankard
four elements earth, air, fire and water

She loves me sure; the cunning of her passion
Invites me in this churlish messenger.   20
None of my lord's ring? Why, he sent her none;
I am the man; if it be so, as 'tis,
Poor lady, she were better love a dream.
Disguise, I see thou art a wickedness,
Wherein the pregnant enemy does much.   25
How easy is it for the proper-false
In women's waxen hearts to set their forms!
Alas, our frailty is the cause, not we,
For such as we are made of, such we be.
How will this fadge? My master loves her dearly,   30
And I (poor monster) fond as much on him
As she (mistaken) seems to dote on me.
What will become of this? As I am man,
My state is desperate for my master's love;
As I am woman – now alas the day!   35
What thriftless sighs shall poor Olivia breathe?
O time, thou must untangle this, not I;
It is too hard a knot for me t'untie.   [*Exit*]

ACT 2   SCENE 3
A room in Olivia's house

Enter SIR TOBY *and* SIR ANDREW

SIR TOBY Approach, Sir Andrew. Not to be abed after midnight is to
be up betimes, and *diluculo surgere*, thou know'st –

SIR ANDREW Nay, by my troth, I know not; but I know to be up late
is to be up late.

SIR TOBY A false conclusion: I hate it as an unfilled can. To be up after   5
midnight and to go bed then is early; so that to go to bed after
midnight is to go to bed betimes. Does not our lives consist of the
four elements?

SIR ANDREW Faith, so they say, but I think it rather consists of eating
and drinking.   10

Feste mimics Sir Andrew's stupidity, but Sir Andrew enjoys the joke and calls for a song. At Sir Toby's request, Feste sings a love song.

---

1 'We Three' (in groups of three)

In Shakespeare's time, a painting showing two asses (fools) was a popular inn sign. The spectator was the third fool! Design a modern version of the inn sign.

In some productions, Feste is given some 'business' (actions) to illustrate 'We Three', for example, sitting alongside the other two and pulling a face. Talk together about what other things Feste might do, then act out your own version of this business.

2 Taking the mickey (in pairs)

It looks as if Feste is mocking Sir Andrew without Sir Andrew realising it. 'Pigrogromitus', 'Vapians' and 'Queubus' are all Shake-speare's nonsense inventions. Some learned critics have tried to make sense out of Feste's lines 23–5. Others think that they are nonsense, and Feste is simply laughing at Sir Andrew (and at learned people!).

Talk together about whether you think lines 23–5 can make sense. Your guess is as good as anyone's! Note that 'I did impeticos thy gratillity' does have a kind of sense about it, as it could be Feste's way of saying 'thank you'.

3 Song (in small groups)

Experiment with different ways of singing Feste's poignant, bitter-sweet song.

---

stoup jug
catch song, round (where each
  singer 'catches' a previous tune or
  word)
breast voice
sooth truth

leman sweetheart
whipstock whip handle
Myrmidons soldiers of Achilles (a
  famous Greek warrior)
testril sixpence
still always

SIR TOBY Th'art a scholar; let us therefore eat and drink. Marian, I
say, a stoup of wine!

Enter CLOWN [FESTE]

SIR ANDREW Here comes the fool, i'faith.

FESTE How now, my hearts? Did you never see the picture of 'We
Three'?   15

SIR TOBY Welcome, ass. Now let's have a catch.

SIR ANDREW By my troth, the fool has an excellent breast. I had rather
than forty shillings I had such a leg, and so sweet a breath to sing,
as the fool has. In sooth, thou wast in very gracious fooling last
night, when thou spok'st of Pigrogromitus, of the Vapians passing   20
the equinoctial of Queubus. 'Twas very good, i'faith: I sent thee
sixpence for thy leman; hadst it?

FESTE I did impeticos thy gratillity: for Malvolio's nose is no whipstock;
my lady has a white hand, and the Myrmidons are no bottle-ale
houses.   25

SIR ANDREW Excellent! Why this is the best fooling, when all is done.
Now a song.

SIR TOBY Come on, there is sixpence for you. Let's have a song.

SIR ANDREW There's a testril of me, too; if one knight give a –

FESTE Would you have a love song or a song of good life?   30

SIR TOBY A love song, a love song.

SIR ANDREW Ay, ay. I care not for good life.

(*Clown* [*Feste*] *sings*)

> O mistress mine, where are you roaming?
> O stay and hear, your true love's coming,
> 　　That can sing both high and low.   35
> Trip no further, pretty sweeting;
> Journeys end in lovers meeting,
> 　　Every wise man's son doth know.

SIR ANDREW Excellent good, i'faith.

SIR TOBY Good, good.   40

FESTE [*Sings*]　　What is love? 'Tis not hereafter;
> 　　Present mirth hath present laughter;
> 　　　　What's to come is still unsure.
> 　　In delay there lies no plenty,
> 　　Then come kiss me, sweet and twenty;   45
> 　　　　Youth's a stuff will not endure.

The three men sing together. Maria pleads with them to be quiet, but they carry on regardless. Malvolio enters and rebukes the revellers.

---

1 Making sense of Sir Toby

'Cataian', 'politicians', and 'Peg-a-Ramsey', might mean 'Chinese', 'schemers' and 'spoil-sport'. But on the other hand, they might be just the nonsense inventions of a drunken man. What do you think?

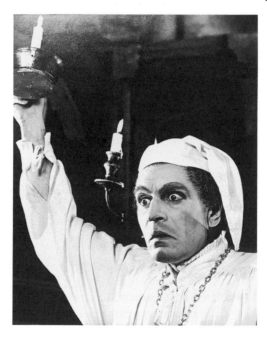

Malvolio's entrance is an invitation to every actor playing the part to astonish and amuse the audience. Draw or describe your image of Malvolio, called out of bed to stop the party.

---

mellifluous honey-like
contagious infectious, evil-smelling (Sir Toby implies that Feste has bad breath)
dulcet sweet
welkin sky
dog/dogs expert/grips (Feste is punning again)

constrain'd ordered, commanded
caterwauling wailing like a cat
consanguineous related by blood
Beshrew me curse me
tinkers menders of pots and pans
coziers shoemakers
mitigation or remorse softening
Sneck up! buzz off!

SIR ANDREW A mellifluous voice, as I am true knight.

SIR TOBY A contagious breath.

SIR ANDREW Very sweet, and contagious, i'faith.

SIR TOBY To hear by the nose, it is dulcet in contagion. But shall we   50
make the welkin dance indeed? Shall we rouse the night owl in a
catch that will draw three souls out of one weaver? Shall we do
that?

SIR ANDREW And you love me, let's do't: I am dog at a catch.

FESTE By'r lady, sir, and some dogs will catch well.   55

SIR ANDREW Most certain. Let our catch be, 'Thou knave'.

FESTE 'Hold thy peace, thou knave', knight? I shall be constrain'd in't
to call thee knave, knight.

SIR ANDREW 'Tis not the first time I have constrained one to call me
knave. Begin, fool. It begins, 'Hold thy peace.'   60

FESTE I shall never begin if I hold my peace.

SIR ANDREW Good, i'faith. Come, begin.

(Catch sung)

Enter MARIA

MARIA What a caterwauling do you keep here! If my lady have not
called up her steward Malvolio and bid him turn you out of doors,
never trust me.   65

SIR TOBY My lady's a Cataian, we are politicians, Malvolio's a
Peg-a-Ramsey, and [*Sings*] 'Three merry men be we.' Am not I
consanguineous? Am I not of her blood? Tilly vally! 'Lady!'
[*Sings*] 'There dwelt a man in Babylon, lady, lady.'

FESTE Beshrew me, the knight's in admirable fooling.   70

SIR ANDREW Ay, he does well enough if he be disposed, and so do I,
too; he does it with a better grace, but I do it more natural.

SIR TOBY [*Sings*] O'the twelfth day of December –

MARIA For the love o'God, peace!

Enter MALVOLIO

MALVOLIO My masters, are you mad? Or what are you? Have you no   75
wit, manners, nor honesty but to gabble like tinkers at this time
of night? Do ye make an alehouse of my lady's house, that ye squeak
out your coziers' catches without any mitigation or remorse of
voice? Is there no respect of place, persons, nor time in you?

SIR TOBY We did keep time, sir, in our catches. Sneck up!   80

Malvolio tells Sir Toby that Olivia wishes him to reform or leave her house. Sir Toby mocks Malvolio, who leaves, threatening Maria. She advises Sir Toby to behave, and begins to tell of her plan to trick Malvolio.

1 Mocking Malvolio (in groups of four)

Sir Toby and Feste sing an old song to annoy Malvolio, refusing to take him seriously. Sir Toby forcefully reminds Malvolio of his inferior social status: 'Go, sir, rub your chain with crumbs' (as Olivia's steward, Malvolio would wear a chain of office – see page 22).

Take parts and act out the Malvolio episode in lines 75–105. Malvolio must try to remain dignified throughout, but Sir Toby should be as irritating as possible, with support from Feste. Maria must decide to what extent she will join in. Afterwards, talk together about whether or not you think Malvolio is being fairly treated. Is he just a killjoy, or does he have a good case?

2 Cakes and ale (in small groups)

In Shakespeare's time, puritans hated the festivities and celebrations that went on at Christmas and Easter. Many puritans thought it was just an excuse to overeat and get drunk. 'Cakes and ale' is Sir Toby's metaphor for enjoyment and celebration.

Either: Work out two tableaux (frozen pictures) to show, in turn, Sir Toby's view and Malvolio's view of 'cakes and ale'.

Or: Write a poem or song to mock Malvolio entitled 'Cakes and ale'.

3 Malvolio's story (in pairs)

Improvise Malvolio's report to Olivia on what has happened. Do it in character!

---

round blunt
nothing allied to totally rejects
ginger spice for ale
give means . . . rule provide drinks for this disorderly party
the field to a duel
indignation angry challenge

gull trick
an ayword a famous fool
common recreation laughing-stock to everyone
puritan strait-laced killjoy

MALVOLIO Sir Toby, I must be round with you. My lady bade me tell you that, though she harbours you as her kinsman, she's nothing allied to your disorders. If you can separate yourself and your misdemeanours, you are welcome to the house; if not, and it would please you to take leave of her, she is very willing to bid you farewell.   85

SIR TOBY [*Sings*] Farewell, dear heart, since I must needs be gone.

MARIA Nay, good Sir Toby.

FESTE [*Sings*] His eyes do show his days are almost done.

MALVOLIO Is't even so?

SIR TOBY [*Sings*] But I will never die.   90

FESTE [*Sings*] Sir Toby, there you lie.

MALVOLIO This is much credit to you.

SIR TOBY [*Sings*] Shall I bid him go?

FESTE [*Sings*] What and if you do?

SIR TOBY [*Sings*] Shall I bid him go, and spare not?   95

FESTE [*Sings*] O no, no, no, no, you dare not.

SIR TOBY Out o'time, sir? Ye lie! Art any more than a steward? Dost thou think because thou art virtuous there shall be no more cakes and ale?

FESTE Yes, by St Anne, and ginger shall be hot i'th'mouth too.   100
[*Exit*]

SIR TOBY Th'art i'th'right. Go, sir, rub your chain with crumbs. A stoup of wine, Maria!

MALVOLIO Mistress Mary, if you prized my lady's favour at anything more than contempt, you would not give means for this uncivil rule; she shall know of it, by this hand.   *Exit*   105

MARIA Go shake your ears.

SIR ANDREW 'Twere as good a deed as to drink when a man's a-hungry, to challenge him the field, and then to break promise with him, and make a fool of him.

SIR TOBY Do't, knight. I'll write thee a challenge, or I'll deliver thy   110
indignation to him by word of mouth.

MARIA Sweet Sir Toby, be patient for tonight. Since the youth of the count's was today with my lady, she is much out of quiet. For Monsieur Malvolio, let me alone with him. If I do not gull him into an ayword, and make him a common recreation, do not   115
think I have wit enough to lie straight in my bed. I know I can do it.

SIR TOBY Possess us, possess us, tell us something of him.

MARIA Marry, sir, sometimes he is a kind of puritan.

SIR ANDREW O if I thought that, I'd beat him like a dog!   120

Maria criticises Malvolio's self-importance and reveals her plan. She will write him a love letter, supposedly from Olivia. Malvolio's vanity will make a fool of him. Sir Toby again attempts to get more of Sir Andrew's money.

1 'Exquisite'

A very difficult word for a drunken man to say! Try speaking it as Sir Toby and Sir Andrew. Perhaps Sir Toby means 'exact'.

2 Planning the trick (in groups of three)

Take parts as Maria, Sir Toby and Sir Andrew. Put your heads as close together as you can, and whisper lines 124–48 to each other as if you are a group of conspirators plotting Malvolio's downfall. Afterwards, talk together about alternative ways of speaking the lines.

3 What is Malvolio like? (in pairs)

Maria lists how she sees Malvolio:

'a time-pleaser' – a time-server or sycophant (creep)
'an affectioned ass' – an affected fool
'that cons state . . . swarths' – who learns high-sounding jargon by heart and quotes it endlessly
'the best persuaded of himself' – think he's wonderful
'so crammed . . . excellencies' – with every desirable quality
'that it is . . . love him' – believes everyone loves him

Take each description in turn and present two mimes for each:
- as Maria sees Malvolio
- as Malvolio sees himself.

4 'I was adored once, too'

Many directors use line 153 to make the audience feel sympathy towards Sir Andrew. How would you advise the actor to speak it?

---

epistles letters
gait walk
device trick
a horse of that colour just that
physic medicine, drug
Penthesilea queen of the Amazons (tall, fierce warrior-women)

beagle small hunting dog
recover win (marry)
'cut' fool, horse without a tail, or female genitals
sack wine, sherry

SIR TOBY What, for being a puritan? Thy exquisite reason, dear knight?

SIR ANDREW I have no exquisite reason for't, but I have reason good
enough.

MARIA The devil a puritan that he is, or anything constantly but a
time-pleaser, an affectioned ass, that cons state without book and   125
utters it by great swarths. The best persuaded of himself: so
crammed (as he thinks) with excellencies, that it is his grounds of
faith that all that look on him love him; and on that vice in him
will my revenge find notable cause to work.

SIR TOBY What wilt thou do?   130

MARIA I will drop in his way some obscure epistles of love, wherein
by the colour of his beard, the shape of his leg, the manner of his
gait, the expressure of his eye, forehead, and complexion, he shall
find himself most feelingly personated. I can write very like my lady
your niece; on a forgotten matter we can hardly make distinction   135
of our hands.

SIR TOBY Excellent, I smell a device.

SIR ANDREW I have't in my nose, too.

SIR TOBY He shall think by the letters that thou wilt drop that they
come from my niece, and that she's in love with him.   140

MARIA My purpose is indeed a horse of that colour.

SIR ANDREW And your horse now would make him an ass.

MARIA Ass, I doubt not.

SIR ANDREW O 'twill be admirable!

MARIA Sport royal, I warrant you: I know my physic will work with   145
him. I will plant you two, and let the fool make a third, where he
shall find the letter. Observe his construction of it. For this night,
to bed, and dream on the event. Farewell.   *Exit*

SIR TOBY Good night, Penthesilea.

SIR ANDREW Before me, she's a good wench.   150

SIR TOBY She's a beagle, true bred, and one that adores me. What
o'that?

SIR ANDREW I was adored once, too.

SIR TOBY Let's to bed, knight. Thou hadst need send for more money.

SIR ANDREW If I cannot recover your niece, I am a foul way out.   155

SIR TOBY Send for money, knight; if thou hast her not i'th'end, call
me 'cut'.

SIR ANDREW If I do not, never trust me; take it how you will.

SIR TOBY Come, come, I'll go burn some sack; 'tis too late to go to
bed now. Come, knight, come, knight.   160

Exeunt

Orsino calls for music to cheer him up, and sends for Feste. Orsino then claims that he is the model of all true lovers, because Olivia is constantly in his thoughts.

1 Soulful music (in groups of five)

Lines 13–20 are very 'poetic'. Shakespeare gives them a musical background. Two of you speak the lines to each other. The other three provide an appropriate musical backing, such as humming gently, or quietly singing a love song. Experiment by changing parts. Find the version you like best.

2 'True lovers'?

Has Orsino got it right, or is he just deceiving himself?

● Talk together about whether you agree that 'true lovers' always have a 'constant image' of their beloved in mind.

● What 'constant image' do you think Orsino really has in mind – Olivia or himself?

● What is your definition of a 'true lover'?

3 Every picture tells a story

Theatre is a very powerful medium of communication, because spoken words are accompanied by physical images. Even actors who do not speak can convey a rich variety of meanings through the way in which they stand, move and relate to others on stage.

Viola does not speak until line 19. But what is she doing up to that point? Write a set of notes to help her to express her thoughts and feelings.

---

light airs trivial tunes
recollected terms artificial words
pangs sufferings, pains
unstaid and skittish unstable and
 playful

all motions else all other emotions
save except
constant image unchanging vision
seat heart

ACT 2 SCENE 4
Orsino's palace

Enter DUKE ORSINO, VIOLA, CURIO, and Lords and Musicians

ORSINO Give me some music –
                [*Musicians step forward*]
                      Now good morrow, friends;
    Now, good Cesario – but that piece of song,
    That old and antique song we heard last night;
    Methought it did relieve my passion much,
    More than light airs and recollected terms   5
    Of these most brisk and giddy-pacèd times.
    Come, but one verse.
CURIO He is not here, so please your lordship, that should sing it.
ORSINO Who was it?
CURIO Feste, the jester, my lord, a fool that the Lady Olivia's father   10
    took much delight in. He is about the house.
ORSINO Seek him out, and play the tune the while.
                            [*Exit Curio*]

          (*Music plays*)
    Come hither, boy; if ever thou shalt love,
    In the sweet pangs of it, remember me:
    For such as I am, all true lovers are,   15
    Unstaid and skittish in all motions else,
    Save in the constant image of the creature
    That is beloved. How dost thou like this tune?
VIOLA It gives a very echo to the seat
    Where love is throned.

Orsino advises Viola that women should marry men older than themselves, because men are fickle, and women soon lose their looks. He asks Feste to sing an old song of love.

1 Shakespeare's autobiography? (whole class)

Was Shakespeare thinking of his own marriage when he wrote lines 27–39? He married Anne Hathaway, who was eight years older than him. Orsino advises Viola that a woman should marry a man older than herself. She will thus be able to keep her husband's affection even though men's emotions are more unstable than women's, and women's beauty quickly fades. Organise a class debate, arguing for and against these three motions:

a Shakespeare was thinking of his own experience in marriage.
b Orsino's advice is good advice.
c Men are more fickle than women.

2 Rural England (in pairs)

Orsino calls for a song. He uses an image that Shakespeare could have seen and heard in Stratford-upon-Avon: women outside their cottages spinning flax or wool, and young girls weaving with bone bobbins, all singing at their work. Or he could be remembering what he saw as he walked from his lodgings in the City of London to the Globe on Bankside: the Huguenots, refugees from France, who became lacemakers and clothworkers.

- Read lines 41–6 to yourself three or four times. Then close your eyes and try to call up in your mind's eye the picture they evoke.
- Debate whether or not you think lines 41–6 are sincere, or just the dreamy fantasies of a self-indulgent, rich man, in love with the idea of being in love and quite out of touch with reality.

---

stayed upon some favour seen a face
i'faith? truly?
worn frayed, worn out
hold the bent stand the strain (like a bent longbow), stay constant

spinsters women who spin flax or wool
free maids carefree girls
silly sooth simple truth
dallies plays

ORSINO   Thou dost speak masterly.   20
    My life upon't, young though thou art, thine eye
    Hath stayed upon some favour that it loves;
    Hath it not, boy?
VIOLA   A little, by your favour,
ORSINO What kind of woman is't?
VIOLA   Of your complexion.
ORSINO She is not worth thee then. What years, i'faith?   25
VIOLA About your years, my lord.
ORSINO Too old, by heaven! Let still the woman take
    An elder than herself; so wears she to him;
    So sways she level in her husband's heart;
    For, boy, however we do praise ourselves,   30
    Our fancies are more giddy and unfirm,
    More longing, wavering, sooner lost and worn,
    Than women's are.
VIOLA   I think it well, my lord.
ORSINO Then let thy love be younger than thyself,
    Or thy affection cannot hold the bent: 35
    For women are as roses, whose fair flower,
    Being once displayed, doth fall that very hour.
VIOLA And so they are. Alas, that they are so:
    To die, even when they to perfection grow!

          Enter CURIO *and* CLOWN [FESTE]

ORSINO O fellow, come, the song we had last night.   40
    Mark it, Cesario, it is old and plain;
    The spinsters and the knitters in the sun,
    And the free maids that weave their thread with bones,
    Do use to chant it; it is silly sooth,
    And dallies with the innocence of love   45
    Like the old age.
FESTE Are you ready, sir?
ORSINO Ay, prithee sing.

53

Feste sings a sad song about a true lover who died for love. He leaves,
commenting on Orsino's changeable moods. Orsino instructs Viola to tell
Olivia that he loves not her wealth, but her beauty.

1 Sad song (in small groups)

Feste's song is about a melancholy lover who dies for love and wants
to be forgotten. Cypress and yew trees were traditionally associated
with death. They were, and still are, found in many churchyards.
Coffins were often made of cypress wood ('sad cypress').

- Make up your own music, or explore ways of speaking the song
  dramatically.
- Work out what everyone on stage does while Feste sings.

2 Mocking Orsino? (in pairs)

Talk together about whether you think Feste's song about a melancholy lover is mocking Orsino, who is himself a melancholy lover. Do
you think Feste is also mocking Orsino in lines 70–4? To help your
thinking, experiment with different ways of speaking the lines. Does
Feste speak directly to Orsino, to members of the court, or to himself?

3 I love you, not your money (in pairs)

That's the message (lines 75–82) Orsino orders Viola to carry to
Olivia, 'yond same sovereign cruelty'. Try the following activity to
bring out Orsino's concern about choosing what he thinks are the
right words to express his feelings. One person reads the lines aloud.
The other echoes every high-flown phrase (for example, 'sovereign
cruelty', 'more noble than the world').

  Afterwards, work out what advice you would give the actor. Suggest
how, in speech and action, he could express Orsino's character
through these eight lines.

Come away come hither
Fie away fly away
My part . . . share it I'm the truest
  lover who ever died for love
strown thrown (strewed)
melancholy god Saturn (whose
  planet was thought to rule
  melancholy people)

taffeta silk which changes colour
opal a jewel which seems to change
  colour
give place leave us
yond yonder
parts gifts
pranks adorns, beautifies

(Music) The Song

Come away, come away, death,
And in sad cypress let me be laid.   50
Fie away, fie away, breath,
I am slain by a fair cruel maid;
    My shroud of white, stuck all with yew,
      O prepare it.
    My part of death no one so true   55
      Did share it.
Not a flower, not a flower sweet,
On my black coffin let there be strown;
Not a friend, not a friend greet
My poor corpse, where my bones shall be thrown: 60
    A thousand thousand sighs to save,
      Lay me, O where
    Sad true lover never find my grave,
      To weep there.

ORSINO There's for thy pains. [*Gives money*]   65
FESTE No pains, sir, I take pleasure in singing, sir.
ORSINO I'll pay thy pleasure then.
FESTE Truly, sir, and pleasure will be paid, one time or another.
ORSINO Give me now leave to leave thee.
FESTE Now the melancholy god protect thee, and the tailor make thy   70
doublet of changeable taffeta, for thy mind is a very opal. I would
have men of such constancy put to sea, that their business might
be everything and their intent everywhere, for that's it that always
makes a good voyage of nothing. Farewell.   *Exit*
ORSINO Let all the rest give place.
            [*Curio and attendants retire*]
                Once more, Cesario,   75
Get thee to yond same sovereign cruelty.
Tell her my love, more noble than the world,
Prizes not quantity of dirty lands;
The parts that fortune hath bestowed upon her
Tell her I hold as giddily as fortune;   80
But 'tis that miracle and queen of gems
That nature pranks her in attracts my soul.
VIOLA But if she cannot love you, sir?
ORSINO I cannot be so answered.

Orsino claims that his capacity for love is greater than that of any woman. Viola, hinting at her own love for Orsino, says tht women love as deeply as men, and that men boast about being in love.

Viola's hints of her love for Orsino present every actor playing the Duke with a problem: how should he respond? Does he simply not notice, or does he begin to suspect that his servant Cesario is not quite what 'he' seems? Is Orsino unsettled by Viola's words? Discuss how you would advise Orsino to respond as Viola speaks lines 101–19.

1 'Patience on a monument' (in small groups or individually)

Either devise a tableau (a frozen picture) to show Viola's image, *or* draw what 'Patience on a monument,/Smiling at grief' suggests to you.

Sooth in truth
pang of heart lovesickness
bide endure
motion of the liver passionate feeling
palate taste only

surfeit, cloyment, and revolt over-eating, discomfort and being sick
damask pink
Our shows . . . will men claim more than they feel
still always
denay denial

VIOLA   Sooth, but you must.
  Say that some lady, as perhaps there is,   85
  Hath for your love as great a pang of heart
  As you have for Olivia. You cannot love her.
  You tell her so. Must she not then be answered?
ORSINO There is no woman's sides
  Can bide the beating of so strong a passion   90
  As love doth give my heart; no woman's heart
  So big, to hold so much. They lack retention.
  Alas, their love may be called appetite,
  No motion of the liver, but the palate,
  That suffers surfeit, cloyment, and revolt,   95
  But mine is all as hungry as the sea,
  And can digest as much. Make no compare
  Between that love a woman can bear me,
  And that I owe Olivia.
VIOLA   Ay, but I know –
ORSINO What dost thou know?   100
VIOLA Too well what love women to men may owe.
  In faith, they are as true of heart as we.
  My father had a daughter loved a man
  As it might be perhaps, were I a woman,
  I should your lordship.
ORSINO   And what's her history? 105
VIOLA A blank, my lord. She never told her love,
  But let concealment like a worm i'th'bud
  Feed on her damask cheek. She pined in thought,
  And with a green and yellow melancholy
  She sat like Patience on a monument,   110
  Smiling at grief. Was not this love indeed?
  We men may say more, swear more, but indeed
  Our shows are more than will: for still we prove
  Much in our vows, but little in our love.
ORSINO But died thy sister of her love, my boy?   115
VIOLA I am all the daughters of my father's house,
  And all the brothers, too – and yet I know not.
  Sir, shall I to this lady?
ORSINO   Ay, that's the theme.
  To her in haste; give her this jewel; say   120
  My love can give no place, bide no denay.

               Exeunt

Sir Toby and Fabian look forward to tricking Malvolio. Maria orders the men to hide and sets the trap for Malvolio: the forged letter.

1 Tricking Malvolio (in groups of five)

Scene 5 makes delightfully funny theatre. To gain a first impression of how Malvolio is gulled (tricked) by his own self-love, take parts as Sir Toby, Sir Andrew, Fabian, Maria and Malvolio. Read quickly through the whole scene. Don't pause – just go for it and enjoy it!

2 Who is Fabian?

Malvolio has reported Fabian to Olivia for bear-baiting (a cruel 'sport' in which a bear, chained to a post, was attacked by dogs). So Fabian is in disgrace. But just who is he? A servant or a gentleman hanger-on of some sort? Invent Fabian's biography (and what he looks like and how he's dressed). Use the tiny clue that he has organised a bear-baiting at Olivia's – what kind of man would do that?

3 Any ideas?

No one is quite sure about exactly what a 'sheep-biter' is. Make a list of what this insulting 'label' could mean, and how it could apply to Malvolio.

4 Show! (in pairs)

Show your partner what a 'contemplative idiot' looks like.

---

scruple tiny part
niggardly stingy, mean
exult rejoice
metal of India pure gold
box-tree evergreen shrub

Close hide
tickling flattery (trout can be caught by gently stroking them to lull them into a false sense of security)

ACT 2 SCENE 5
Olivia's garden

Enter SIR TOBY, SIR ANDREW and FABIAN

SIR TOBY Come thy ways, Signior Fabian.

FABIAN Nay, I'll come. If I lose a scruple of this sport, let me be boiled
to death with melancholy.

SIR TOBY Wouldst thou not be glad to have the niggardly rascally
sheep-biter come by some notable shame?   5

FABIAN I would exult, man. You know he brought me out o'favour with
my lady about a bear-baiting here.

SIR TOBY To anger him, we'll have the bear again; and we will fool
him black and blue, shall we not, Sir Andrew?

SIR ANDREW And we do not, it is pity of our lives.   10

SIR TOBY Here comes the little villain.

Enter MARIA

How now, my metal of India?

MARIA Get ye all three into the box-tree. Malvolio's coming down this
walk. He has been yonder i'the sun practising behaviour to his own
shadow this half hour. Observe him, for the love of mockery, for   15
I know this letter will make a contemplative idiot of him. Close,
in the name of jesting!

[The men hide]

Lie thou there [*Drops a letter*]; for here comes the trout that must
be caught with tickling.   *Exit*

Malvolio day-dreams aloud, persuading himself that Olivia loves him, and imagining that they are married. Sir Toby and Sir Andrew are enraged.

---

1 She and me (in pairs)

One person reads aloud Malvolio's lines 20–4. Every time he refers to himself or Olivia ('I', 'she', and so on), the other person says loudly 'Malvolio' or 'Olivia'. You'll discover how much Malvolio has Olivia (and himself!) on his mind.

2 Overhearing: how do they hide?

Every director of the play seizes the challenge of 'the box-tree' (literally, an evergreen shrub), and aims to make this overhearing scene as hilarious as possible. There's a huge amount of potential laughter in how Sir Toby and his friends hide. They are always on the brink of being seen by Malvolio, but just manage to avoid discovery. In different productions they have hidden behind benches, trees, hedges, statues, walls and windows. Sometimes they have even posed as garden statues!

Work out how you would stage this scene to greatest comic effect.

3 'The Lady of the Strachy'

Nobody knows just who Shakespeare had in mind when Malvolio mentions the Lady who married beneath her ('the yeoman of the wardrobe' is a servant). Invent her story.

4 Ways of looking

Try imitating two of Malvolio's ways of looking superior:

lines 44–5 'demure travel of regard' (a cool look at the servants)
line 55 'austere regard of control' (a cold and superior stare).

---

fortune luck, destiny
affect admire
fancy love
overweening immensely conceited
jets struts

advanced plumes puffed-out feathers (like a turkey-cock)
'Slight by God's light (an oath)
Jezebel shameless woman
stone-bow catapult
branched embroidered

Enter MALVOLIO

MALVOLIO 'Tis but fortune; all is fortune. Maria once told me she did   20
  affect me, and I have heard herself come thus near, that should she
  fancy, it should be one of my complexion. Besides, she uses me with
  a more exalted respect than any one else that follows her. What
  should I think on't?

SIR TOBY Here's an overweening rogue!   25

FABIAN O peace! Contemplation makes a rare turkey-cock of him; how
  he jets under his advanced plumes!

SIR ANDREW 'Slight, I could so beat the rogue!

FABIAN Peace, I say!

MALVOLIO To be Count Malvolio!   30

SIR TOBY Ah, rogue!

SIR ANDREW Pistol him, pistol him!

FABIAN Peace, peace!

MALVOLIO There is example for't: the Lady of the Strachy married
  the yeoman of the wardrobe –   35

SIR ANDREW Fie on him, Jezebel!

FABIAN O peace! Now he's deeply in. Look how imagination blows him.

MALVOLIO Having been three months married to her, sitting in my state –

SIR TOBY O for a stone-bow to hit him in the eye!

MALVOLIO Calling my officers about me, in my branched velvet gown,   40
  having come from a day-bed, where I have left Olivia sleeping –

SIR TOBY Fire and brimstone!

FABIAN O peace, peace!

MALVOLIO And then to have the humour of state; and after a demure
  travel of regard – telling them I know my place, as I would they   45
  should do theirs – to ask for my kinsman Toby –

SIR TOBY Bolts and shackles!

FABIAN O peace, peace, peace! Now, now.

MALVOLIO Seven of my people, with an obedient start, make out for
  him. I frown the while, and perchance wind up my watch, or play   50
  with my – some rich jewel. Toby approaches; curtsies there to me –

SIR TOBY Shall this fellow live?

FABIAN Though our silence be drawn from us by th'ears, yet peace!

MALVOLIO I extend my hand to him thus, quenching my familiar smile
  with an austere regard of control –   55

SIR TOBY And does not 'Toby' take you a blow o'the lips then?

Malvolio discovers the letter and thinks that he recognises the handwriting as Olivia's. He tries to figure out the contents.

Which line opposite do you think best fits this moment? Prepare your own version of Malvolio's letter-reading. Give him plenty of time to puzzle out the meaning – it makes the scene even funnier.

1 Very rude!

Shakespeare put a crude joke into lines 72–5. Elizabethans knew that 'cut' was slang for the female genitals, and they would hear 'P's' as 'pees'. They would probably find it very funny that Sir Andrew fails to see the dirty joke. In modern productions, directors have to decide what to do with the lines. What would you do?

prerogative right
sinews strength
woodcock near the gin bird near the trap
the spirit . . . intimate the god of emotions suggests
in contempt of without
impressure stamp

Lucrece seal-ring (representing Lucrece, the model of chastity)
Jove king of the gods (see page 165)
numbers verses, metre
brock badger
gore wound
fustian bombastic, pretentious

MALVOLIO Saying, 'Cousin Toby, my fortunes having cast me on your
    niece, give me this prerogative of speech – '
SIR TOBY What, what?
MALVOLIO 'You must amend your drunkenness.'   60
SIR TOBY Out, scab!
FABIAN Nay, patience, or we break the sinews of our plot.
MALVOLIO 'Besides, you waste the treasure of your time with a foolish
    knight – '
SIR ANDREW That's me, I warrant you.   65
MALVOLIO 'One Sir Andrew – '
SIR ANDREW I knew 'twas I, for many do call me fool.
MALVOLIO [*Taking up the letter*] What employment have we here?
SIR TOBY Now is the woodcock near the gin.
FABIAN O peace, and the spirit of humours intimate reading aloud to 70
    him!
MALVOLIO By my life, this is my lady's hand: these be her very c's,
    her u's, and her t's, and thus makes she her great P's. It is, in
    contempt of question, her hand.
SIR ANDREW Her c's, her u's, and her t's: why that?   75
MALVOLIO [*Reads*] 'To the unknown beloved, this, and my good
    wishes' – her very phrases! By your leave, wax. Soft! And the
    impressure her Lucrece, with which she uses to seal: 'tis my lady.
    To whom should this be? [*Opens the letter*]
FABIAN This wins him, liver and all.   80
MALVOLIO [*Reads*]   Jove knows I love,
                  But who?
                Lips, do not move:
                No man must know.
    'No man must know.' What follows? The numbers altered! 'No   85
    man must know'! If this should be thee, Malvolio!
SIR TOBY Marry, hang thee, brock!
MALVOLIO [*Reads*]   I may command where I adore,
                  But silence, like a Lucrece knife,
                  With bloodless stroke my heart doth gore;   90
                  M.O.A.I. doth sway my life.
FABIAN A fustian riddle!
SIR TOBY Excellent wench, say I.
MALVOLIO 'M.O.A.I. doth sway my life.' Nay, but first let me see, let
    me see, let me see.   95

Twelfth Night

*Malvolio persuades himself that Olivia has written the poem to him. He
reads what follows: that he should transform himself from a steward into a
great gentleman.*

1 Hawking and hunting

Sir Toby and Fabian use images from Elizabethan field sports as they
comment on Malvolio's puzzlement:

> 'with what wing . . . at it' – how quickly the kestrel flies mistakenly
> at it
> 'cold scent' – the hounds have lost the fox
> 'Sowter will cry' – the hound (named Sowter) will bark
> 'excellent at faults' – can find the fox when the scent is lost.

Invent gestures to accompany each image to make its meaning clear.

2 Reading the letter (in small groups)

Lines 118–32 give every actor playing Malvolio a great chance to
entertain the audience. Most read the letter slowly, sentence by
sentence. They leave long pauses in which they can insert much stage
business, milking the speech for laughs. For example, at 'revolve'
(line 119), one Malvolio slowly turned round and round with
increasing glee, as if he had made a great discovery.

- Work on the letter sentence by sentence. Create appropriate stage
  business for each sentence or phrase that you think would entertain
  the audience.

- What do the overhearers do as Malvolio reads? They'll certainly be
  finding it hard to stop laughing. But imagine that they put on a little
  show for each other to illustrate each sentence of the letter, and
  mock Malvolio at the same time. Work out their parody that takes
  place behind Malvolio's back.

---

dressed prepared
formal capacity normal
  intelligence
rank smelly
no consonancy . . . probation no
  consistency that stands up to test
detraction disasters
simulation appearance

inure accustom
cast thy humble slough get rid of
  your humble manner (like a snake
  casting off its old skin)
tang . . . state speak loudly about
  politics
the trick of singularity distinctive
  behaviour and dress

FABIAN What dish o'poison has she dressed him!

SIR TOBY And with what wing the staniel checks at it!

MALVOLIO 'I may command where I adore.' Why, she may command me: I serve her; she is my lady. Why, this is evident to any formal capacity. There is no obstruction in this, and the end – what should that alphabetical position portend? If I could make that resemble something in me – Softly! 'M.O.A.I.' –

SIR TOBY O ay, make up that! He is now at a cold scent.

FABIAN Sowter will cry upon't for all this, though it be as rank as a fox.

MALVOLIO 'M' – Malvolio. 'M' – why, that begins my name!

FABIAN Did not I say he would work it out? The cur is excellent at faults.

MALVOLIO 'M' – but then there is no consonancy in the sequel that suffers under probation. 'A' should follow, but 'O' does.

FABIAN And O shall end, I hope.

SIR TOBY Ay, or I'll cudgel him and make him cry 'O'!

MALVOLIO And then 'I' comes behind.

FABIAN Ay, and you had any eye behind you, you might see more detraction at your heels than fortunes before you.

MALVOLIO 'M.O.A.I.' This simulation is not as the former, and yet, to crush this a little, it would bow to me, for every one of these letters are in my name. Soft, here follows prose. [*Reads*] 'If this fall into thy hand, revolve. In my stars I am above thee, but be not afraid of greatness. Some are born great, some achieve greatness, and some have greatness thrust upon 'em. Thy fates open their hands; let thy blood and spirit embrace them, and, to inure thyself to what thou art like to be, cast thy humble slough and appear fresh. Be opposite with a kinsman, surly with servants; let thy tongue tang arguments of state; put thyself into the trick of singularity. She thus advises thee that sighs for thee. Remember who commended thy yellow stockings and wished to see thee ever cross-gartered: I say, remember. Go to, thou art made if thou desir'st to be so; if not, let me see thee a steward still, the fellow of servants, and not worthy to touch Fortune's fingers. Farewell. She that would alter services with thee,

                                    The Fortunate-Unhappy.'

Malvolio is overjoyed. He will follow the instructions in every detail – even smiling! The conspirators are ecstatic about the success of their plot.

---

1 Malvolio is delighted (in pairs)

Malvolio's joy knows no bounds. The trick has worked, and Malvolio is caught in the net of his own self-importance. Explore ways of speaking lines 133–47 to find the most entertaining presentation. Here are some suggestions to help you work out a final version:

a One person reads. The other echoes every 'I', 'me', 'my'.

b Echo and emphasise every verb: 'discovers', 'is', 'will be' . . .

c Create a gesture or action for every sentence or phrase.

d Read the postscript to the letter (lines 143–6) in different ways, for example: very fast, with increasing delight, or with great puzzlement.

e Turn the lines into a conversation. Each partner reads alternate sentences or phrases.

f One partner reads each sentence (or part of a sentence) as a question. The other repeats it immediately as a very emphatic statement.

g *'Exit'*. How does Malvolio leave the stage? Practise different ways in which he might go off. Decide the style you most prefer to give the audience maximum enjoyment.

2 Poor Sir Andrew (in pairs)

Read aloud everything Sir Andrew says in the script opposite. Also say the line immediately before each of Sir Andrew's sentences. What do you think his constant repetitions suggest about his character?

---

champain open country
baffle humiliate
point-device in every detail
jade deceive, trick
injunction order
habits clothes
strange, stout aloof, proud

Jove king of the gods (see page 165)
sophy shah of Persia (see page 100)
dowry marriage gift
tray-trip a dice game (won by throwing a three)
acqua-vitae brandy
Tartar hell

Daylight and champain discovers not more! This is open. I will be
proud, I will read politic authors, I will baffle Sir Toby, I will wash
off gross acquaintance, I will be point-device, the very man. I do   135
not now fool myself to let imagination jade me; for every reason
excites to this, that my lady loves me. She did commend my yellow
stockings of late, she did praise my leg being cross-gartered; and
in this she manifests herself to my love, and with a kind of
injunction drives me to these habits of her liking. I thank my stars,   140
I am happy. I will be strange, stout, in yellow stockings, and
cross-gartered, even with the swiftness of putting on. Jove and my
stars be praised! Here is yet a postscript. [*Reads*] 'Thou canst not
choose but know who I am. If thou entertain'st my love, let it appear
in thy smiling; thy smiles become thee well. Therefore in my   145
presence still smile, dear my sweet, I prithee.' Jove, I thank thee.
I will smile; I will do every thing that thou wilt have me.   *Exit*

FABIAN I will not give my part of this sport for a pension of thousands
    to be paid from the sophy.
SIR TOBY I could marry this wench for this device –   150
SIR ANDREW So could I, too.
SIR TOBY And ask no other dowry with her but such another jest.
SIR ANDREW Nor I neither.
FABIAN Here comes my noble gull-catcher.

Enter MARIA

SIR TOBY Wilt thou set thy foot o'my neck?   155
SIR ANDREW Or o'mine either?
SIR TOBY Shall I play my freedom at tray-trip and become thy
    bondslave?
SIR ANDREW I'faith, or I either?
SIR TOBY Why, thou hast put him in such a dream that when the image   160
    of it leaves him, he must run mad.
MARIA Nay, but say true, does it work upon him?
SIR TOBY Like acqua-vitae with a midwife.
MARIA If you will then see the fruits of the sport, mark his first approach
    before my lady. He will come to her in yellow stockings, and 'tis   165
    a colour she abhors, and cross-gartered, a fashion she detests; and
    he will smile upon her, which will now be so unsuitable to her
    disposition, being addicted to a melancholy as she is, that it cannot
    but turn him into a notable contempt. If you will see it, follow me.
SIR TOBY To the gates of Tartar, thou most excellent devil of wit!   170
SIR ANDREW I'll make one, too.   *Exeunt*

67

Looking back at Act 2
Activities for groups or individuals

1 Five scenes, five places

The five scenes of Act 2 are set on the sea-coast, a street outside Olivia's house, inside Olivia's house, at Duke Orsino's and in Olivia's garden. Work out how you would ensure that the action on stage flows smoothly from scene to scene, without interruption or long delays for scene-shifting.

2 Singing the catch

In Scene 3, the tipsy merrymakers sing several songs, beginning with a catch (a song where each singer repeats a phrase from the previous singer). Try different ways of singing the catch, making up your own music but using the repeated lines: 'Hold thy peace, thou knave'. Sir Toby also sings fragments of other songs popular in Shakespeare's day. Choose one of them, make up a few more lines, and practise your own Elizabethan song:

a 'Three merry men be we'
b 'There dwelt a man in Babylon, lady, lady'
c 'O' the twelfth day of December'.

3 Maria: 'My niece's chambermaid'

Sir Toby describes Maria as 'little villain', and 'metal of India'. He jokes twice about her height, calling her first 'Penthesilea' (Queen of the Amazons, a race of tall, fierce warrior-women), and then 'beagle' (a small hunting dog). Viola pleads 'Some mollification for your giant, sweet lady' as Maria tries to persuade her to leave Olivia's house.

Talk together about whether it would increase audience amusement to cast a tall or a short actor as Maria. Consider who could play Maria (from people you have seen on television or on stage) – and why.

4 Different viewpoints on romantic love

To gain a quite different view of the discussion of love between Orsino and Viola, try this activity, working in groups of four. Two of you are Orsino and Viola. The other two are palace cleaners, on your hands and knees scrubbing the floor. Orsino and Viola read lines 75–121 from Scene 4, pausing frequently. They are totally oblivious of the cleaners, who are scrubbing away near their feet. The cleaners hear everything, and comment loudly to each other on all that's said. You'll find it gives quite a different slant on love!

Sir Toby and his allies watch Malvolio swallow the bait. In some productions, they have crawled frantically around the stage to avoid discovery as Malvolio strolls about, obsessed by his thoughts. In one production, Sir Andrew became a garden bench and Malvolio sat on him!

Decide where you could stage the gulling scene in the open air somewhere around your school or college. One college production had the conspirators dodging among the dustbins – and sometimes jumping into them.

Feste juggles with words, declining to give Viola a straight answer. He comments sceptically on the slipperiness of language and on the foolishness of husbands.

1 Feste: 'her corrupter of words'

Feste's joking and punning arises from the slipperiness of language: 'words are very rascals' (line 17) and 'words are grown so false' (lines 20–1). Feste enjoys playing with different meanings of the same word (for example 'live' = 'earn money' or 'have a house'). Yet he jokingly accuses Viola of doing just the same – twisting words to give them different meanings ('A sentence is but a cheveril glove to a good wit', lines 9–10).

When Feste says that words have become unreliable 'since bonds (promises) disgraced them', he is probably pointing once again to the way in which a word can change its meaning. Promises are made of words, but because words can be interpreted differently, it's difficult to keep promises.

Save thee may God preserve you (traditional greeting)
tabor small side-drum
cheveril soft leather

dally nicely play cleverly
wanton loose, disreputable, unchaste
bonds promises

ACT 3 SCENE 1
In Olivia's orchard

Enter VIOLA *and* FESTE, *playing on a pipe and tabor*

VIOLA Save thee, friend, and thy music! Dost thou live by thy tabor?

FESTE No, sir, I live by the church.

VIOLA Art thou a churchman?

FESTE No such matter, sir. I do live by the church; for I do live at my
house, and my house doth stand by the church.   5

VIOLA So thou mayst say the king lies by a beggar, if a beggar dwell
near him; or the church stands by thy tabor if thy tabor stand by
the church.

FESTE You have said, sir. To see this age! A sentence is but a cheveril
glove to a good wit – how quickly the wrong side may be turned   10
outward!

VIOLA Nay, that's certain: they that dally nicely with words may
quickly make them wanton.

FESTE I would therefore my sister had had no name, sir.

VIOLA Why, man?   15

FESTE Why, sir, her name's a word, and to dally with that word might
make my sister wanton; but, indeed, words are very rascals, since
bonds disgraced them.

VIOLA Thy reason, man?

FESTE Truth, sir, I can yield you none without words, and words are   20
grown so false, I am loath to prove reason with them.

VIOLA I warrant thou art a merry fellow and car'st for nothing.

FESTE Not so, sir, I do care for something; but in my conscience, sir,
I do not care for you: if that be to care for nothing, I would it would
make you invisible.   25

VIOLA Art not thou the Lady Olivia's fool?

FESTE No, indeed, sir. The Lady Olivia has no folly. She will keep no
fool, sir, till she be married, and fools are as like husbands as
pilchards are to herrings – the husband's the bigger. I am indeed
not her fool but her corrupter of words.   30

Feste, still juggling with words, talks Viola into giving him money. She reflects on the need for fools to be clever. Sir Toby invites Viola to visit Olivia.

1 Shakespeare the playwright (in small groups)

Shakespeare was at the very centre of the theatrical life in Elizabethan times. His plays often contain references to the theatre:

Pandarus, Cressida, Troilus, (lines 43–4) Shakespeare's *Troilus and Cressida* is a play about two young lovers, set during the siege of Troy by the Greeks. Pandarus was the Trojan lord who acted as go-between for the ill-starred young lovers.

'Elements' Shakespeare may be defending a fellow playwright, Ben Jonson, who was attacked for his fondness for using the word 'element'. Talk together about what someone means when they say 'it's out of my element'.

A tribute to an actor? Lines 50–8 may be Shakespeare's tribute to Robert Armin, the actor who first played Feste. Talk together about the general sense of the lines, namely that the really good joker ('wise fool') suits his humour to the particular audience and occasion, rather than cracking jokes about everything. It will help your discussion to use modern comedians as examples.

Speaking French Lines 61–2 mean 'God save you sir'/'And you also; your servant'. Why do you think Shakespeare uses French here?

Dramatic irony A powerful technique much used by Shakespeare (see page 164). Viola's aside (line 40) is a great opportunity to make the audience laugh or smile. Advise the actor how to speak it.

---

late recently
orb earth
your wisdom 'your worship'
and thou pass upon if you joke about
conster explain (construe)
out of my welkin unknown to me

craves demands
haggard wild, untamed hawk
check fly at
fit appropriate
folly-fall'n behaving foolishly
Save you God save you
list objective, purpose

VIOLA I saw thee late at the Count Orsino's.

FESTE Foolery, sir, does walk about the orb like the sun; it shines everywhere. I would be sorry, sir, but the fool should be as oft with your master as with my mistress: I think I saw your wisdom there.   35

VIOLA Nay, and thou pass upon me, I'll no more with thee. Hold, there's expenses for thee. [*Gives a coin*]

FESTE Now Jove, in his next commodity of hair, send thee a beard!

VIOLA By my troth, I'll tell thee, I am almost sick for one – [*Aside*] though I would not have it grow on my chin. Is thy lady within?   40

FESTE Would not a pair of these have bred, sir?

VIOLA Yes, being kept together and put to use.

FESTE I would play Lord Pandarus of Phrygia, sir, to bring a Cressida to this Troilus.

VIOLA I understand you sir; 'tis well begged. [*Gives another coin*]   45

FESTE The matter, I hope, is not great, sir – begging but a beggar: Cressida was a beggar. My lady is within, sir. I will conster to them whence you come. Who you are, and what you would are out of my welkin – I might say 'clement', but the word is overworn.

Exit

VIOLA This fellow is wise enough to play the fool,   50
And to do that well craves a kind of wit;
He must observe their mood on whom he jests,
The quality of persons, and the time;
Not, like the haggard, check at every feather
That comes before his eye. This is a practice,   55
As full of labour as a wise man's art:
For folly that he wisely shows is fit;
But wise men, folly-fall'n, quite taint their wit.

Enter SIR TOBY *and* [SIR] ANDREW

SIR TOBY Save you, gentleman.

VIOLA And you, sir.   60

SIR ANDREW *Dieu vous garde, monsieur.*

VIOLA *Et vous aussi; votre serviteur.*

SIR ANDREW I hope, sir, you are, and I am yours.

SIR TOBY Will you encounter the house? My niece is desirous you should enter, if your trade be to her.   65

VIOLA I am bound to your niece, sir; I mean, she is the list of my voyage.

Viola-Cesario gives punning replies to Sir Toby. Sir Andrew is impressed by Viola-Cesario's elegant language. Olivia begins to reveal her true feelings to Viola-Cesario.

1 Punning is infectious (in pairs)

Viola has just experienced Feste's playfulness with language. Now she is quick to make similar puns in answer to Sir Toby's mocking. One person reads lines 68–9 and 71. The other makes appropriate gestures to highlight the puns on 'understand' and 'gait'.

2 Sir Andrew responds

Viola addresses Olivia in highly elaborate, courteous speech. Her compliments greatly impress Sir Andrew. Advise the actor playing Sir Andrew how he should behave at each of the following moments:

a As he says: 'well' (line 73): impressed? contemptuous?

b 'I'll get 'em all three' (lines 76–7): memorises? writes down?

c When Olivia says 'leave me' (line 78): how does Sir Andrew exit with Maria and Sir Toby? willingly? reluctant to go? or . . . ? (Remember he's only visiting Sir Toby in order to woo Olivia, and he's probably not had a chance even to talk with her.)

3 'Music from the spheres'

Many Elizabethans believed that the planets were contained in concentric crystal spheres which rotated, creating wonderfully harmonious music that could not be heard by humans. If Shakespeare were writing today, what modern comparison might he substitute for line 95, 'music from the spheres'?

Taste try out
gait step (or gate)
odours perfume
pregnant ready
vouchsafed willing

lowly feigning pretended humility
blanks empty
whet sharpen, tempt
suit cause
solicit plead for, entreat

SIR TOBY Taste your legs, sir; put them to motion.
VIOLA My legs do better understand me, sir, than I understand what
    you mean by bidding me taste my legs.
SIR TOBY I mean, to go, sir, to enter.   70
VIOLA I will answer you with gait and entrance – but we are prevented.

Enter OLIVIA *and* GENTLEWOMAN [MARIA]

Most excellent accomplished lady, the heavens rain odours on you!
SIR ANDREW That youth's a rare courtier – 'rain odours' – well.
VIOLA My matter hath no voice, lady, but to your own most pregnant
    and vouchsafed ear.   75
SIR ANDREW 'Odours', 'pregnant', and 'vouchsafed': I'll get 'em all
    three all ready.
OLIVIA Let the garden door be shut, and leave me to my hearing.
                    [*Exeunt Sir Toby, Sir Andrew, and Maria*]
    Give me your hand, sir.
VIOLA My duty, madam, and most humble service.   80
OLIVIA What is your name?
VIOLA Cesario is your servant's name, fair princess.
OLIVIA My servant, sir? 'Twas never merry world
    Since lowly feigning was called compliment.
    Y'are servant to the Count Orsino, youth.   85
VIOLA And he is yours, and his must needs be yours:
    Your servant's servant is your servant, madam.
OLIVIA For him, I think not on him; for his thoughts,
    Would they were blanks, rather than filled with me!
VIOLA Madam, I come to whet your gentle thoughts   90
    On his behalf.
OLIVIA   O by your leave, I pray you!
    I bade you never speak again of him;
    But would you undertake another suit
    I had rather hear you to solicit that,
    Than music from the spheres.
VIOLA   Dear lady –   95
OLIVIA Give me leave, beseech you. I did send,
    After the last enchantment you did here,
    A ring in chase of you. So did I abuse
    Myself, my servant, and, I fear me, you.

Olivia hints at the agonies of love she feels. She says her feelings are clearly visible. After seeming to dismiss Viola-Cesario, Olivia calls her back. Viola-Cesario declares that she is not what she seems.

1 Love and cruelty

Bear-baiting (see page 58) In lines 103–5, Olivia uses the image of bear-baiting ('stake', 'baited' and 'unmuzzled') to describe how her secret love for Viola-Cesario tears at her. Make a drawing to illustrate Olivia's image of being chained and baited like a bear by the 'unmuzzled thoughts' of Viola-Cesario's cruel heart.

Lions and wolves Just who does Olivia have in mind in line 114? Does she think of Viola-Cesario as the lion (king of men) or the wolf (cruel predator)? Talk together about your own views. Might she be also thinking of Orsino?

2 Monosyllables (in pairs)

Simple, short words can be charged with meaning and have great dramatic effect. Read lines 122–9 to each other, but accompany each monosyllabic word (a word with only one syllable) with a stamp of your foot, or tap on the table. Try this several times. Then work out a way of saying the lines so that they do not sound staccato (like the rat-a-tat-tat of a machine-gun). Or would you want them to sound like that?

3 'I am not what I am'

In Shakespeare's time, line 126 would have been spoken by a boy playing a girl playing a boy. That fact made the words rich in dramatic irony (see page 164). Today the part of Viola is played by a woman, but the line is still full of dramatic irony, because the audience knows what Olivia does not – the 'man' she is wooing is actually a woman.

---

hard construction harsh
 judgement
receiving perception
cypress thin linen
degree step
grise step

vulgar proof common experience
upbraids rebukes
westward ho! the cry of London
 boatmen offering to carry
 passengers from the City to
 Westminster (see page 162)

Under your hard construction must I sit,   100
To force that on you in a shameful cunning
Which you knew none of yours. What might you think?
Have you not set mine honour at the stake,
And baited it with all th'unmuzzled thoughts
That tyrannous heart can think? To one of your receiving   105
Enough is shown; a cypress, not a bosom,
Hides my heart: so, let me hear you speak.

VIOLA I pity you.

OLIVIA   That's a degree to love.

VIOLA No, not a grise; for 'tis a vulgar proof
That very oft we pity enemies.   110

OLIVIA Why then, methinks 'tis time to smile again.
O world, how apt the poor are to be proud!
If one should be a prey, how much the better
To fall before the lion than the wolf!
            (*Clock strikes*)
The clock upbraids me with the waste of time.   115
Be not afraid, good youth; I will not have you –
And yet when wit and youth is come to harvest,
Your wife is like to reap a proper man.
There lies your way, due west.

VIOLA   Then westward ho!
Grace and good disposition attend your ladyship!   120
You'll nothing, madam, to my lord by me?

OLIVIA Stay!
I prithee tell me what thou think'st of me.

VIOLA That you do think you are not what you are.

OLIVIA If I think so, I think the same of you.   125

VIOLA Then think you right: I am not what I am.

OLIVIA I would you were as I would have you be.

VIOLA Would it be better, madam, than I am?
I wish it might, for now I am your fool.

Olivia, admiring Viola's beauty and convinced that her own feelings are obvious, declares her love for Viola-Cesario. Viola swears that no woman has her heart except she herself.

Which line do you think is being spoken?

1 Style matches meaning

Try different ways of speaking (lines 142–7) to find if you agree with the following interpretation:

'Viola's meaning and feelings are absolutely straightforward and sincere, so Shakespeare gives her words and a style to match. In contrast, Olivia expresses a difficult idea in lines 138–41, so Shakespeare provides her with a convoluted style of speaking to match her thoughts – don't twist the fact that I'm wooing you to mean you shouldn't love me, but argue it this way ('reason thus with reason fetter'): loving is good, but receiving love is better.'

Love's night is noon love cannot be hidden	**clause** proposition
maugre in spite of	**For that** because
extort extract	**fetter** chain up
	deplore declare, complain about

OLIVIA [*Aside*] O what a deal of scorn looks beautiful   130
    In the contempt and anger of his lip!
    A murd'rous guilt shows not itself more soon,
    Than love that would seem hid. Love's night is noon.
    Cesario, by the roses of the spring,
    By maidhood, honour, truth, and everything,   135
    I love thee so that, maugre all thy pride,
    Nor wit nor reason can my passion hide.
    Do not extort thy reasons from this clause,
    For that I woo, thou therefore hast no cause;
    But rather reason thus with reason fetter: 140
    Love sought is good, but giv'n unsought is better.
VIOLA By innocence I swear, and by my youth,
    I have one heart, one bosom, and one truth,
    And that no woman has; nor never none
    Shall mistress be of it, save I alone.   145
    And so, adieu, good madam; never more
    Will I my master's tears to you deplore.
OLIVIA Yet come again: for thou perhaps mayst move
    That heart which now abhors to like his love.

                              Exeunt

Sir Andrew determines to leave because Olivia is paying more attention to Viola-Cesario. Fabian and Sir Toby persuade him to stay. He must challenge Viola-Cesario to a duel and so win Olivia's affection by his bravery.

'No, faith, I'll not stay a jot longer!' Sir Andrew and Sir Toby, Royal Shakespeare Company, 1979.

1 Echoes of Elizabethan England

In Shakespeare's day, the audience would have picked up references made to recent events (see also page 162):

- 'hang like an icicle on a Dutchman's beard' (lines 21–2): Olivia's cold indifference and frosty disdain is compared to a voyage made to the Arctic in 1596–7 by a Dutchman, William Barents.
- 'Brownist' (line 25): a follower of the puritan, Robert Brown.

venom fury	**fire-new from the mint** like brand-new coins
Marry by St Mary	
great argument clear show	**balked** let slip, neglected
'Slight! by God's light	**double gilt** goldplated twice
dormouse sleeping, timid	**valour** bravery
accosted greeted	**policy** cunning, trickery
	as lief as gladly

Act 3   Scene 2
A room in Olivia's house

Enter SIR TOBY, SIR ANDREW and FABIAN

SIR ANDREW No, faith, I'll not stay a jot longer!

SIR TOBY Thy reason, dear venom, give thy reason.

FABIAN You must needs yield your reason, Sir Andrew.

SIR ANDREW Marry, I saw your niece do more favours to the count's
servingman than ever she bestowed upon me. I saw't i'th'orchard.   5

SIR TOBY Did she see thee the while, old boy? Tell me that.

SIR ANDREW As plain as I see you now.

FABIAN This was a great argument of love in her toward you.

SIR ANDREW 'Slight! Will you make an ass o'me?

FABIAN I will prove it legitimate, sir, upon the oaths of judgement and   10
reason.

SIR TOBY And they have been grand-jurymen since before Noah was
a sailor.

FABIAN She did show favour to the youth in your sight only to
exasperate you, to awake your dormouse valour, to put fire in your   15
heart, and brimstone in your liver. You should then have accosted
her, and with some excellent jests, fire-new from the mint, you
should have banged the youth into dumbness. This was looked for
at your hand, and this was balked. The double gilt of this
opportunity you let time wash off, and you are now sailed into the   20
north of my lady's opinion, where you will hang like an icicle on
a Dutchman's beard unless you do redeem it by some laudable
attempt, either of valour or policy.

SIR ANDREW And't be any way, it must be with valour, for policy I
hate. I had as lief be a Brownist as a politician.   25

SIR TOBY Why then, build me thy fortunes upon the basis of valour.
Challenge me the count's youth to fight with him, hurt him in eleven
places – my niece shall take note of it – and assure thyself, there
is no love-broker in the world can more prevail in man's commen-
dation with woman than report of valour.   30

Sir Toby instructs Sir Andrew how to write the challenge in fierce, military language, but tells Fabian that Sir Andrew is a coward. Maria brings news that Malvolio has been transformed!

1 'Thou' and 'you'

To Elizabethans, words like 'thou', 'thy' and 'thee' were very significant. 'Thou' was used for a close friend, but could also be used insultingly to someone you did not like or treated as an inferior. 'You' was a more distant way of speaking to someone. Check how Sir Toby and Fabian address Sir Andrew throughout the scene (as 'thou' or 'you'). How do you explain the difference?

2 Sir Toby: truth or trick? (in pairs)

Sir Toby is a mischief-maker. Although he pretends to be Sir Andrew's friend, he continually mocks and tricks him. But sometimes Sir Toby reveals his true thoughts (for example, 'I have been dear to him' – I've spent his money). One person reads aloud everything Sir Toby says in this scene, a sentence at a time. Pause at the end of each sentence. The other person says either 'mischief' or 'truth' in each pause. Change roles and repeat.

3 More contemporary echoes

- 'The bed of Ware' (line 37) was a huge bed that could sleep a dozen people. It is now in the Victoria and Albert Museum, London.

- 'the new map . . . Indies' (lines 62–3): a map of India and the Far East published in 1600. It had lines which radiated out from different points like wrinkles around the eyes.

Research one of the contemporary echoes above or one of those on page 162. Present your findings together with a comment on what you think such Elizabethan references add to the play.

---

curst fierce	**hale** haul, drag
invention imagination (or untruths)	**presage** hint
	spleen fit of laughter
goose-pen quill-pen (or cowardly)	**gull** dupe, tricked person
cubiculo bedroom	**passages of grossness** written nonsense
dear manikin friendly puppet	
wainropes wagon ropes	**pedant** schoolmaster

FABIAN There is no way but this, Sir Andrew.

SIR ANDREW Will either of you bear me a challenge to him?

SIR TOBY Go, write it in a martial hand, be curst and brief; it is no
matter how witty, so it be eloquent, and full of invention. Taunt
him with the licence of ink. If thou 'thou'st' him some thrice, it   35
shall not be amiss, and as many lies as will lie in thy sheet of paper,
although the sheet were big enough for the bed of Ware in England,
set 'em down. Go, about it! Let there be gall enough in thy ink;
though thou write with a goose-pen, no matter. About it!

SIR ANDREW Where shall I find you?   40

SIR TOBY We'll call thee at the cubiculo. Go!

                                                        Exit Sir Andrew

FABIAN This is a dear manikin to you, Sir Toby.

SIR TOBY I have been dear to him, lad, some two thousand strong, or
so.

FABIAN We shall have a rare letter from him, but you'll not deliver't?   45

SIR TOBY Never trust me then, and by all means stir on the youth to
an answer. I think oxen and wainropes cannot hale them together.
For Andrew, if he were opened and you find so much blood in his
liver as will clog the foot of a flea, I'll eat the rest of th'anatomy.

FABIAN And his opposite, the youth, bears in his visage no great presage   50
of cruelty.

                                Enter MARIA

SIR TOBY Look where the youngest wren of mine comes –

MARIA If you desire the spleen, and will laugh yourselves into stitches,
follow me. Yond gull Malvolio is turned heathen, a very renegado;
for there is no Christian that means to be saved by believing rightly   55
can ever believe such impossible passages of grossness. He's in
yellow stockings.

SIR TOBY And cross-gartered?

MARIA Most villainously. Like a pedant that keeps a school i'th'church.
I have dogged him like his murderer. He does obey every point of   60
the letter that I dropped to betray him. He does smile his face into
more lines than is in the new map with the augmentation of the
Indies; you have not seen such a thing as 'tis. I can hardly forbear
hurling things at him; I know my lady will strike him. If she do,
he'll smile and take't for a great favour.   65

SIR TOBY Come bring us, bring us where he is.

                                                             Exeunt

Twelfth Night

Antonio has followed Sebastian out of friendship and to protect him.
Sebastian invites Antonio to join him in sightseeing. Antonio declines,
fearing capture – he was once Orsino's enemy.

Choose a line from the script
opposite which you think best
fits this moment.

1 Antonio and Sebastian

Imagine the two actors ask your advice:

a 'When we look at lines 1–18, Antonio seems to care for Sebastian
  more than Sebastian cares for him. Just how should we play the
  lines?'
b 'Antonio is a wanted man in Illyria. How does he show by his
  manner that he's taking a considerable risk? How does Sebastian
  react to that manner?'

Advise them on each point in as much detail as you can.

chide rebuke
jealousy fear
befall endanger
skilless in without knowledge
the rather the more speedily (the
  original meaning of 'rather')
shuffled off poorly rewarded

uncurrent worthless
relics famous buildings
the count his galleys Orsino's
  ships
tane captured (taken)
scarce be answered be difficult to
  avoid punishment

ACT 3   SCENE 3
A street

Enter SEBASTIAN and ANTONIO

SEBASTIAN I would not by my will have troubled you,
    But since you make your pleasure of your pains,
    I will no further chide you.
ANTONIO I could not stay behind you. My desire,
    More sharp than filèd steel, did spur me forth;   5
    And not all love to see you (though so much
    As might have drawn one to a longer voyage),
    But jealousy what might befall your travel,
    Being skilless in these parts which to a stranger,
    Unguided, and unfriended, often prove   10
    Rough and unhospitable. My willing love,
    The rather by these arguments of fear,
    Set forth in your pursuit.
SEBASTIAN   My kind Antonio,
    I can no other answer make but thanks,
    And thanks, and ever thanks; and oft good turns   15
    Are shuffled off with such uncurrent pay;
    But were my worth, as is my conscience, firm,
    You should find better dealing. What's to do?
    Shall we go see the relics of this town?
ANTONIO Tomorrow, sir; best first go see your lodging.   20
SEBASTIAN I am not weary, and 'tis long to night.
    I pray you, let us satisfy our eyes
    With the memorials and the things of fame
    That do renown this city.
ANTONIO   Would you'd pardon me.
    I do not without danger walk these streets.   25
    Once in a sea-fight 'gainst the count his galleys
    I did some service, of such note indeed
    That were I tane here, it would scarce be answered.

Antonio is a wanted man in Illyria because he has not repaid what he captured in a sea-fight. He lends Sebastian money. The two men promise to meet later at the Elephant.

1 Who is Antonio?

Antonio is a wanted man in Illyria because of a sea-fight between the ships of his city and those of Duke Orsino. All his fellow citizens have made their peace with Orsino by returning what they captured in the battle. Only Antonio has refused to settle.

a Design a 'wanted' poster of Antonio to be displayed on walls around Illyria.

b Compile the official Illyrian document that records full details of Antonio's life.

c Write the Illyrian battle report of the sea-fight.

d Invent a story to explain why Antonio thinks the Elephant is a safe place to stay. Has he been there before? What do you think lies behind his words 'best to lodge' (line 40)?

2 The Elephant (in groups of three)

The Elephant was an inn very close to the Globe theatre. Shakespeare probably passed it every day on his way to the theatre. It has long since disappeared. The reference is not to the area of London now known as Elephant and Castle, as it was not called that in Shakespeare's time.

Was Shakespeare giving free publicity to the inn? Talk together about whether you think Shakespeare's choice of name has genuine significance, or is just a random choice.

3 'I'll be your purse-bearer'

Watch out for the trouble this loan of money (line 47) causes later in the play!

Belike perhaps
traffic's trade's
stood out did not pay
lapsèd arrested
It doth not fit me I'll be cautious

bespeak our diet order our meal
Haply maybe
toy trifling object
store . . . markets money is
insufficient for buying luxuries

SEBASTIAN Belike you slew great number of his people?
ANTONIO Th'offence is not of such a bloody nature,   30
       Albeit the quality of the time and quarrel
       Might well have given us bloody argument.
       It might have since been answered in repaying
       What we took from them, which for traffic's sake
       Most of our city did. Only myself stood out,   35
       For which if I be lapsèd in this place
       I shall pay dear.
SEBASTIAN   Do not then walk too open.
ANTONIO It doth not fit me. Hold, sir, here's my purse.
       In the south suburbs at the Elephant
       Is best to lodge; I will bespeak our diet,   40
       Whiles you beguile the time, and feed your knowledge
       With viewing of the town; there shall you have me.
SEBASTIAN Why I your purse?
ANTONIO Haply your eye shall light upon some toy
       You have desire to purchase; and your store,   45
       I think, is not for idle markets, sir.
SEBASTIAN I'll be your purse-bearer and leave you for
       An hour.
ANTONIO   To th'Elephant.
SEBASTIAN   I do remember.

                              Exeunt

Olivia is looking forward to Viola-Cesario's return, and thinking about how she will entertain 'him'. She sends for Malvolio, expecting him to be formal and sad. He appears – transformed and speaking very strangely!

1 She's talking about you! (in small groups)

Olivia makes what seems to be a cynical remark about young people in line 3: 'For youth is bought more oft than begged or borrowed' (it's money that counts in winning young people's love). Do you share her view? Discuss her belief, and what her remark makes you think about her character – and her age.

2 Advice, please

The actor playing Olivia says to you 'Line 1 is very odd, because I don't really know if Viola-Cesario will return or not. But the line is "he says he'll come". How do I say that?' Advise her.

3 'Please one, and please all'

Malvolio sings the opening lines of a popular Elizabethan song: 'The Crowe sits upon the Wall/Please one and please all'. Make up four lines to follow which express what's in Malvolio's mind at this moment.

4 Act it out! (in groups of six)

Malvolio's appearance in yellow stockings and cross-gartered is a great moment in every production. Take parts as Olivia, Maria, Malvolio, the Servant, Sir Toby and Fabian and act out lines 1–106.

Remember, Malvolio is convinced that Olivia loves him. Olivia, knowing nothing of the forged letter, is astonished by his appearance and behaviour. The conspirators are beside themselves with glee, and are determined to add to the impression that Malvolio is mad. Get as much fun from the 'mis-takings' as you can!

---

bestow of him give to him
possessed mad, taken over by the devil
sonnet song

black in my mind melancholy
Roman hand fashionable italic handwriting

ACT 3 SCENE 4
Olivia's garden

Enter OLIVIA *followed by* MARIA

OLIVIA [*Aside*] I have sent after him; he says he'll come –
    How shall I feast him? What bestow of him?
    For youth is bought more oft than begged or borrowed.
    I speak too loud –
    Where's Malvolio? He is sad and civil,   5
    And suits well for a servant with my fortunes.
    Where is Malvolio?
MARIA He's coming, madam, but in very strange manner. He is sure
    possessed, madam.
OLIVIA Why, what's the matter? Does he rave?   10
MARIA No, madam, he does nothing but smile. Your ladyship were best
    to have some guard about you, if he come, for sure the man is
    tainted in's wits.
OLIVIA Go call him hither.

                                [*Exit Maria*]

             I am as mad as he
    If sad and merry madness equal be.   15

Enter [MARIA *with*] MALVOLIO

    How now, Malvolio?
MALVOLIO Sweet lady, ho, ho!
OLIVIA Smil'st thou? I sent for thee upon a sad occasion.
MALVOLIO Sad, lady? I could be sad. This does make some obstruction
    in the blood, this cross-gartering, but what of that? If it please the   20
    eye of one, it is with me as the very true sonnet is: 'Please one,
    and please all.'
OLIVIA Why, how dost thou, man? What is the matter with thee?
MALVOLIO Not black in my mind, though yellow in my legs. It did
    come to his hands, and commands shall be executed. I think we   25
    do know the sweet Roman hand.

Olivia is amazed by Malvolio's behaviour and appearance as he quotes the forged letter to her. She thinks he is mad, and gives orders for Sir Toby and others to look after him.

'Midsummer madness.' Malvolio shows off his yellow stockings.

1 Does she mean it?

What does the last sentence spoken by Olivia (lines 56–7) suggest to you about her true feelings for Malvolio?

daws jackdaws
restore cure
commended praised
thou art made you are blessed by
  fortune

could . . . entreat him back I had
great difficulty keeping him out

OLIVIA Wilt thou go to bed, Malvolio?

MALVOLIO To bed? Ay, sweetheart, and I'll come to thee.

OLIVIA God comfort thee! Why dost thou smile so and kiss thy hand
    so oft?   30

MARIA How do you, Malvolio?

MALVOLIO At your request!
    Yes, nightingales answer daws!

MARIA Why appear you with this ridiculous boldness before my lady?

MALVOLIO 'Be not afraid of greatness': 'twas well writ.   35

OLIVIA What mean'st thou by that, Malvolio?

MALVOLIO 'Some are born great – '

OLIVIA Ha?

MALVOLIO 'Some achieve greatness – '

OLIVIA What say'st thou?   40

MALVOLIO 'And some have greatness thrust upon them.'

OLIVIA Heaven restore thee!

MALVOLIO 'Remember who commended thy yellow stockings – '

OLIVIA Thy yellow stockings?

MALVOLIO 'And wished to see thee cross-gartered.'   45

OLIVIA Cross-gartered?

MALVOLIO 'Go to, thou art made, if thou desir'st to be so – '

OLIVIA Am I made?

MALVOLIO 'If not, let me see thee a servant still.'

OLIVIA Why, this is very midsummer madness.   50

Enter SERVANT

SERVANT Madam, the young gentleman of the Count Orsino's is
    returned; I could hardly entreat him back. He attends your
    ladyship's pleasure.

OLIVIA I'll come to him.

                                                  [Exit Servant]

    Good Maria, let this fellow be looked to. Where's my cousin Toby?   55
    Let some of my people have a special care of him; I would not have
    him miscarry for the half of my dowry.

                                     [Exeunt Olivia and Maria]

Malvolio convinces himself that what Olivia has just said means that she loves him. Following the letter's instructions, he is rude to Sir Toby, who accuses him of being possessed by devils.

1 Malvolio deceives himself (in small groups)

Practise saying Malvolio's soliloquy (lines 58–73) to each other to bring out his preening and vanity. Add 'business' (gestures and action) to increase the humour. Perhaps Malvolio hugs himself with joy.

The soliloquy works well as a 'conversation'. Sit in a circle. As Malvolio, each person takes a turn to read a sentence or phrase telling the others how pleased with himself Malvolio is.

2 Tormenting Malvolio (in groups of four)

Sir Toby, Fabian and Maria torment Malvolio with their mock concern in lines 74–106. Take parts. The three conspirators stand around Malvolio. As each conspirator speaks, Malvolio must turn away from them and reply contemptuously. Then try other ways of heightening the comic effect (for example, Sir Toby could make signs to fend off the devil).

3 Legion

Sir Toby and Fabian are determined to treat Malvolio as if he is possessed by devils. 'Legion' (line 75) is mentioned in the Bible (St Mark's Gospel, chapter 5), where Jesus casts out a legion (many thousands) of devils from a madman. Some critics see the image as yet another way in which the play links suffering with love – Malvolio is accused of being mad because he believes that Olivia loves him. Which other characters in *Twelfth Night* do you think suffer for love?

---

humble slough lowly appearance
tang talk pretentiously
singularity eccentricity
reverend carriage stately walk
limed caught (birds were trapped with lime)
Fellow companion (of Olivia)
degree rank (as a servant)

dram tiny weight
scruple even tinier weight (one third of a dram)
sanctity holiness
water urine
wise woman fortune teller (who claimed to be able to diagnose from urine samples)

MALVOLIO O ho, do you come near me now? No worse man than Sir
   Toby to look to me! This concurs directly with the letter: she sends
   him on purpose that I may appear stubborn to him; for she incites   60
   me to that in the letter. 'Cast thy humble slough', says she; 'be
   opposite with a kinsman, surly with servants, let thy tongue tang
   with arguments of state, put thyself into the trick of singularity',
   and consequently sets down the manner how: as a sad face, a
   reverend carriage, a slow tongue, in the habit of some sir of note,   65
   and so forth. I have limed her, but it is Jove's doing, and Jove make
   me thankful! And when she went away now, 'Let this fellow be
   looked to' – 'Fellow'! Not 'Malvolio', nor after my degree, but
   'fellow'. Why, everything adheres together, that no dram of a
   scruple, no scruple of a scruple, no obstacle, no incredulous or   70
   unsafe circumstance – what can be said? Nothing that can be can
   come between me and the full prospect of my hopes. Well, Jove,
   not I, is the doer of this, and he is to be thanked!

   Enter [SIR] TOBY, FABIAN, *and* MARIA

SIR TOBY Which way is he, in the name of sanctity? If all the devils
   of hell be drawn in little, and Legion himself possessed him, yet   75
   I'll speak to him.
FABIAN Here he is, here he is. How is't with you, sir?
SIR TOBY How is't with you, man?
MALVOLIO Go off, I discard you. Let me enjoy my private. Go off!
MARIA Lo, how hollow the fiend speaks within him! Did not I tell you?   80
   Sir Toby, my lady prays you to have a care of him.
MALVOLIO Ah ha! Does she so?
SIR TOBY Go to, go to; peace, peace! We must deal gently with him.
   Let me alone. How do you, Malvolio? How is't with you? What,
   man, defy the devil! Consider, he's an enemy to mankind.   85
MALVOLIO Do you know what you say?
MARIA La you, and you speak ill of the devil, how he takes it at heart!
   Pray God he be not bewitched!
FABIAN Carry his water to th'wise woman.
MARIA Marry, and it shall be done tomorrow morning if I live. My lady   90
   would not lose him for more than I'll say.
MALVOLIO How now, mistress?
MARIA O Lord!

*Sir Toby continues to pretend that Malvolio is mad. Malvolio refuses to be
teased, and leaves. Sir Toby plans to tie him up and put him in prison.
Sir Andrew arrives with his letter of challenge to Viola-Cesario.*

---

1 'If this were played upon a stage . . .'

In the theatre, Fabian's words (lines 108–9) nearly always make the
audience laugh. But the actor has to decide how, and to whom to say
it: to the audience? to the others? to himself? Experiment with ways of
speaking the lines to get the funniest effect. Afterwards, talk together
about why you think Shakespeare inserted the lines.

2 Cluck, cluck

Sir Toby treats Malvolio like a chicken, which has to be encouraged
with endearing terms, like 'bawcock' (fine bird), 'chuck' (chicken) and
'biddy' (chickabiddy). Invent some stage business for Sir Toby to
accompany the lines. For example, does Sir Toby taunt Malvolio by
clucking?

3 Malvolio's feelings (in pairs)

Malvolio's language in lines 79–106 shows that he feels many
different emotions. One person speaks each sentence, pausing after
each. The other person suggests what Malvolio is feeling and
thinking at that moment. Afterwards, talk together about which taunt
offends Malvolio most of all.

4 'In a dark room and bound'

Elizabethans believed that a mad person could be cured by imprison-
ing them in a dark room. Sir Toby is keen to put this cruel 'cure' into
practice with Malvolio. What does this suggest to you about Sir
Toby's character? How do you think Maria and Fabian react to the
suggestion?

'tis not . . . Satan dignified people
  shouldn't play children's games
  with the devil
foul collier dirty digger
genius soul, spirit
take air and taint become known,
  and therefore spoiled

penance confession
bar court
More matter for a May morning!
  more sport fit for a holiday!
keeps you . . . law saves you from
  prosecution

SIR TOBY Prithee, hold thy peace; this is not the way. Do you not see
    you move him? Let me alone with him.   95
FABIAN No way but gentleness; gently, gently: the fiend is rough, and
    will not be roughly used.
SIR TOBY Why, how now, my bawcock? How dost thou, chuck?
MALVOLIO Sir!
SIR TOBY Ay, biddy, come with me. What, man, 'tis not for gravity   100
    to play at cherry-pit with Satan. Hang him, foul collier!
MARIA Get him to say his prayers, good Sir Toby, get him to pray.
MALVOLIO My prayers, minx!
MARIA No, I warrant you, he will not hear of godliness.
MALVOLIO Go hang yourselves all! You are idle, shallow things; I am   105
    not of your element. You shall know more hereafter.   *Exit*
SIR TOBY Is't possible?
FABIAN If this were played upon a stage now, I could condemn it as
    an improbable fiction.
SIR TOBY His very genius hath taken the infection of the device, man.   110
MARIA Nay, pursue him now, lest the device take air and taint.
FABIAN Why, we shall make him mad indeed.
MARIA The house will be the quieter.
SIR TOBY Come, we'll have him in a dark room and bound. My niece
    is already in the belief that he's mad. We may carry it thus for our   115
    pleasure, and his penance, till our very pastime, tired out of breath,
    prompt us to have mercy on him; at which time we will bring the
    device to the bar and crown thee for a finder of madmen. But see,
    but see!

Enter SIR ANDREW

FABIAN More matter for a May morning!   120
SIR ANDREW Here's the challenge; read it. I warrant there's vinegar
    and pepper in't.
FABIAN Is't so saucy?
SIR ANDREW Ay, is't. I warrant him; do but read.
SIR TOBY Give me. [*Reads*] 'Youth, whatsoever thou art, thou art but   125
    a scurvy fellow.'
FABIAN Good, and valiant.
SIR TOBY [*Reads*] 'Wonder not, nor admire not in thy mind, why I do
    call thee so, for I will show thee no reason for't.'
FABIAN A good note! That keeps you from the blow of the law.   130

Sir Toby reads Sir Andrew's contorted letter and orders him to challenge Viola-Cesario forcefully in the orchard. Sir Andrew leaves, and Sir Toby reveals he plans to trick both duellists into mutual fright.

1 Write the challenge

The first audience for *Twelfth Night* probably included many law students (see page 166). They would relish Sir Andrew's attempts to ensure that his letter doesn't land him in court. Write out Sir Andrew's challenge to Viola-Cesario. Add any drawings you feel are appropriate. Try to make Sir Andrew's handwriting reveal his true feelings.

2 'Thou'

Sir Toby earlier (Act 3 Scene 2, lines 35–6) urged Sir Andrew to use 'thou' when speaking to Viola-Cesario. Read the letter aloud emphasising every 'thou', 'thy' and 'thee'. Remind yourself of the Elizabethan custom about 'thou' on page 82.

3 'Like cockatrices' (in pairs)

Cockatrices were mythical serpents, supposed to be able to kill with a look (line 163). Show your partner how to kill like a cockatrice.

4 Another trick

Sir Toby is up to no good yet again. This time he plans to trick both Sir Andrew and Viola-Cesario into believing that the other is a superb swordsman, so that they will be terrified of each other. One person takes the role of Sir Toby. The others question him: 'Why do you do it? Why do you want to humiliate Sir Andrew?'

---

o' th' windy side of the law safe from prosecution
commerce conversation, business
bumbaily bailiff (who approached from behind)
approbation credit

of good capacity and breeding intelligent and noble
clodpole blockhead
set upon attribute to, give
presently immediately
horrid threatening

SIR TOBY [*Reads*] 'Thou com'st to the Lady Olivia, and in my sight she uses thee kindly. But thou liest in thy throat. That is not the matter I challenge thee for.'

FABIAN Very brief, and to exceeding good sense [*Aside*] – less.

SIR TOBY [*Reads*] 'I will waylay thee going home, where if it be thy   135
chance to kill me –'

FABIAN Good.

SIR TOBY [*Reads*] 'Thou kill'st me like a rogue and a villain.'

FABIAN Still you keep o'th'windy side of the law. Good.

SIR TOBY [*Reads*] 'Fare thee well, and God have mercy upon one of   140
our souls! He may have mercy upon mine, but my hope is better, and so look to thyself. Thy friend, as thou usest him, and thy sworn enemy,
                                        Andrew Aguecheek.'

If this letter move him not, his legs cannot. I'll give't him.   145

MARIA You may have very fit occasion for't; he is now in some commerce with my lady and will by and by depart.

SIR TOBY Go, Sir Andrew, scout me for him at the corner of the orchard like a bumbaily. So soon as ever thou seest him, draw, and as thou draw'st, swear horrible; for it comes to pass oft that a terrible oath,   150
with a swaggering accent sharply twanged off, gives manhood more approbation than ever proof itself would have earned him Away!

SIR ANDREW Nay, let me alone for swearing.   *Exit*

SIR TOBY Now will not I deliver his letter; for the behaviour of the young gentleman gives him out to be of good capacity and breeding;   155
his employment between his lord and my niece confirms no less. Therefore this letter, being so excellently ignorant, will breed no terror in the youth; he will find it comes from a clodpole. But, sir, I will deliver his challenge by word of mouth, set upon Aguecheek a notable report of valour, and drive the gentleman (as I know his   160
youth will aptly receive it) into a most hideous opinion of his rage, skill, fury, and impetuosity. This will so fright them both that they will kill one another by the look, like cockatrices.

FABIAN Here he comes with your niece; give them way till he take leave and presently after him.   165

                Enter OLIVIA *and* VIOLA

SIR TOBY I will meditate the while upon some horrid message for a challenge.

                [*Exeunt Sir Toby, Fabian, and Maria*]

Olivia reveals her passionate love to Viola-Cesario, and gives 'him' a jewel. Viola-Cesario tells her to love Orsino instead. Sir Toby tells Viola-Cesario to draw 'his' sword and face Sir Andrew's rage and supreme swordsmanship.

1 What did Olivia say? (in pairs)

At the opening of the scene, Olivia was impatiently awaiting the arrival of Viola-Cesario. Now she enters with 'I have said too much unto a heart of stone' (line 168), and says that she has spoken without caution ('unchary') of her love for 'him'. Improvise the off-stage conversation in which Olivia reveals her love, but Viola-Cesario rejects it.

2 Friend or fiend? (in small groups)

Talk together about whether or not you would change 'friend' (line 184) to 'fiend'.

3 A change of scene

Lines 183–4 are like the rhyming couplets which often end scenes in Shakespeare's plays. If you were directing the play, you could set the rest of this scene in a different location. What do you think are the advantages and disadvantages of changing the location at line 185?

4 Putting on the frighteners (in pairs)

In lines 185–219, Sir Toby paints a picture of a furious and formidable Sir Andrew. Viola is puzzled and probably frightened.

Take parts and read the lines. Change roles and read through again with Viola trying to get away from Sir Toby while he constantly pursues her, emphasising all the violent words.

With the same 'haviour ... griefs
  Orsino suffers in similar manner
acquit release
betake thee to't prepare it
Dismount thy tuck unsheath your
  rapier
yare quick
opposite opponent, enemy

dubbed with unhatched rapier
  made a knight with an unused
  (unhacked) sword
carpet consideration non-military
  service
sepulchre burial
Hob nob have or have not (kill or
  be killed)

OLIVIA I have said too much unto a heart of stone,
　　　And laid mine honour too unchary on't;
　　　There's something in me that reproves my fault,   170
　　　But such a headstrong potent fault it is,
　　　That it but mocks reproof.
VIOLA With the same 'haviour that your passion bears
　　　Goes on my master's griefs.
OLIVIA Here, wear this jewel for me; 'tis my picture.   175
　　　Refuse it not; it hath no tongue to vex you.
　　　And, I beseech you, come again tomorrow.
　　　What shall you ask of me that I'll deny,
　　　That honour, saved, may upon asking give?
VIOLA Nothing but this – your true love for my master.   180
OLIVIA How with mine honour may I give him that
　　　Which I have given to you?
VIOLA 　　　　　　　　　　　I will acquit you.
OLIVIA Well, come again tomorrow. Fare thee well.
　　　A friend like thee might bear my soul to hell.   [*Exit*]

　　　　　Enter SIR TOBY *and* FABIAN

SIR TOBY Gentleman, God save thee.   185
VIOLA And you, sir.
SIR TOBY That defence thou hast, betake thee to't. Of what nature the
wrongs are thou hast done him, I know not; but thy intercepter, full
of despite, bloody as the hunter, attends thee at the orchard-end.
Dismount thy tuck, be yare in thy preparation, for thy assailant is   190
quick, skilful, and deadly.
VIOLA You mistake, sir. I am sure no man hath any quarrel to me. My
remembrance is very free and clear from any image of offence done
to any man.
SIR TOBY You'll find it otherwise, I assure you. Therefore, if you hold   195
your life at any price, betake you to your guard; for your opposite
hath in him what youth, strength, skill, and wrath can furnish man
withal.
VIOLA I pray you, sir, what is he?
SIR TOBY He is knight, dubbed with unhatched rapier, and on carpet   200
consideration, but he is a devil in private brawl. Souls and bodies
hath he divorced three, and his incensement at this moment is so
implacable that satisfaction can be none but by pangs of death and
sepulchre. Hob nob is his word: give't or take't.

Viola tries to avoid the duel, but Sir Toby, then Fabian, prevent her and tell of Sir Andrew's bravery. Sir Toby then similarly frightens Sir Andrew with report of Viola's sword-fencing skill.

1 Sir Andrew – what he's not!

Collect all the words in lines 185–231 which describe Sir Andrew. Copy out and complete the diagram below, putting his name in the centre of a large piece of paper and writing the words from the script around it.

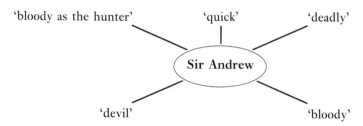

Beside each description write other words which you think describe him more accurately. You could use words and phrases from other parts of the play.

2 'Fencer to the sophy'

In 1600, Sir Anthony Sherley published an account of his adventures whilst serving as ambassador to the shah of Persia ('the sophy'). There was great interest in the autobiography. Shakespeare probably inserted this reference to amuse the audience. Sir Anthony's brother, Robert, was still serving in the shah's army when the play was written.

Draw the image that comes into Sir Andrew's mind when he hears the expression 'fencer to the sophy'.

---

conduct safety
quirk peculiarity, type
competent sufficient, real
meddle get involved
iron sword
mortal arbitrement fight to the
  death

read him by his form judge by his
  appearance
mettle bravery
firago virago (female warrior)
sophy the shah of Persia
Pox on't curse it

VIOLA I will return again into the house and desire some conduct of   205
the lady. I am no fighter. I have heard of some kind of men that
put quarrels purposely on others to taste their valour; belike this
is a man of that quirk.

SIR TOBY Sir, no. His indignation derives itself out of a very competent
injury; therefore get you on and give him his desire. Back you shall   210
not to the house, unless you undertake that with me which with
as much safety you might answer him; therefore on, or strip your
sword stark naked; for meddle you must, that's certain, or forswear
to wear iron about you.

VIOLA This is as uncivil as strange. I beseech you, do me this courteous   215
office as to know of the knight what my offence to him is. It is
something of my negligence, nothing of my purpose.

SIR TOBY I will do so. Signior Fabian, stay you by this gentleman till
my return.   *Exit [Sir] Toby*

VIOLA Pray you, sir, do you know of this matter?   220

FABIAN I know the knight is incensed against you, even to a mortal
arbitrement, but nothing of the circumstance more.

VIOLA I beseech you, what manner of man is he?

FABIAN Nothing of that wonderful promise, to read him by his form,
as you are like to find him in the proof of his valour. He is indeed,   225
sir, the most skilful, bloody, and fatal opposite that you could
possibly have found in any part of Illyria. Will you walk towards
him? I will make your peace with him if I can.

VIOLA I shall be much bound to you for't. I am one that had rather
go with sir priest than sir knight. I care not who knows so much   230
of my mettle.

Exeunt

Enter [SIR] TOBY and [SIR] ANDREW

SIR TOBY Why, man, he's a very devil. I have not seen such a firago.
I had a pass with him, rapier, scabbard, and all, and he gives me
the stuck-in with such a mortal motion that it is inevitable; and on
the answer, he pays you as surely as your feet hits the ground they   235
step on. They say he has been fencer to the sophy.

SIR ANDREW Pox on't. I'll not meddle with him.

SIR TOBY Ay, but he will not now be pacified. Fabian can scarce hold
him yonder.

Andrew promises to give Sir Toby his horse if he can persuade Viola-Cesario to call off the duel. Viola is equally terrified. Sir Toby forces them to draw swords, but Antonio enters and intervenes on Viola's behalf.

1 Staging the duel (in small groups)

Lines 220–63 make wonderfully funny theatre. Both Viola and Sir Andrew are terrified of each other. Fabian and Sir Toby do all they can to heighten the fear. Sometimes the mock fight lasts for two or three minutes as the terrified opponents, spurred on by Sir Toby and Fabian, ludicrously fence with each other. In some productions, they cover their eyes and jump back fearfully at any touch of swords. Viola speaks an aside (lines 255–6) which, with its irony and sexual humour, usually causes great audience amusement.

Take parts (have a director if you wish) and work out how to stage the lines for maximum comic effect. Health warning: don't use real swords or sharp objects!

---

motion offer
perdition of souls loss of life
Marry by St Mary
conceited full of imagined fear

duello rules of duelling
undertaker someone who meddles
  in another's affairs

SIR ANDREW Plague on't, and I thought he had been valiant, and so 240
cunning in fence, I'd have seen him damned ere I'd have challenged
him. Let him let the matter slip, and I'll give him my horse, Grey
Capilet.

SIR TOBY I'll make the motion. Stand here, make a good show on't.
This shall end without the perdition of souls. [*Aside*] Marry, I'll 245
ride your horse as well as I ride you.

Enter FABIAN *and* VIOLA

[*To Fabian*] I have his horse to take up the quarrel. I have
persuaded him the youth's a devil.

FABIAN He is as horribly conceited of him and pants and looks pale,
as if a bear were at his heels. 250

SIR TOBY [*To Viola*] There's no remedy, sir. He will fight with you
for's oath sake. Marry, he hath better bethought him of his quarrel,
and he finds that now scarce to be worth talking of. Therefore, draw
for the supportance of his vow. He protests he will not hurt you.

VIOLA [*Aside*] Pray God defend me! A little thing would make me tell 255
them how much I lack of a man.

FABIAN Give ground if you see him furious.

SIR TOBY Come, Sir Andrew, there's no remedy: the gentleman will
for his honour's sake have one bout with you; he cannot by the
duello avoid it, but he has promised me, as he is a gentleman and 260
a soldier, he will not hurt you. Come on, to't.

SIR ANDREW Pray God he keep his oath!

VIOLA I do assure you, 'tis against my will.

[*They draw*]

Enter ANTONIO

ANTONIO [*Drawing*] Put up your sword! If this young gentleman
Have done offence, I take the fault on me; 265
If you offend him, I for him defy you.

SIR TOBY You, sir? Why, what are you?

ANTONIO One, sir, that for his love dares yet do more
Than you have heard him brag to you he will.

SIR TOBY Nay, if you be an undertaker, I am for you. [*Draws*] 270

Enter OFFICERS

FABIAN O good Sir Toby, hold! Here comes the officers.

Viola-Cesario and Sir Andrew make peace. The officers arrest Antonio. He asks Viola-Cesario for his money, mistaking 'him' for Sebastian. She, puzzled, offers him half her own small amount of money. He finds her ungrateful.

1 'You stand amazed'

Shakespeare often builds stage directions into characters' language. It's no wonder that Viola is bewildered. First she finds herself forced into a duel for no reason she can discover. Then Sir Andrew says something very odd to her, promising her a horse (lines 274–5) she knows nothing about. Now her rescuer, a man she has never seen before, is arrested and asks her to return his money!

Work through lines 274–90 (in which Viola does not speak) and advise Viola how she should react to each line or phrase.

2 'You do mistake me, sir' (in pairs)

Antonio mistakes Viola for Sebastian. One person reads aloud everything Antonio says to Viola pausing at each 'you'. In each pause the other person says 'You do mistake me, sir'. Afterwards, consider each character on stage in turn, and identify which other characters they have mistaken.

3 Monster ingratitude (in small groups)

Shakespeare seems to have hated ingratitude (not being grateful for kindnesses done for you). He refers to it very critically in several plays (*Coriolanus, King Lear, Troilus and Cressida*). Now Antonio accuses Viola of ingratitude. Do you share Viola's judgement (lines 305–8) that ingratitude is more hateful than any other vice? Begin by talking together about the other three vices she mentions.

---

reins wells handles well
office duty
suit order
favour features, appearance
my present my money

coffer purse
deserts claims for past kindnesses
unsound mean-spirited
vainness boasting

SIR TOBY [*To Antonio*] I'll be with you anon.

VIOLA [*To Sir Andrew*] Pray, sir, put your sword up, if you please.

SIR ANDREW Marry, will I, sir; and for that I promised you, I'll be
 as good as my word. He will bear you easily and reins well. 275

1 OFFICER This is the man; do thy office.

2 OFFICER Antonio, I arrest thee at the suit
 Of Count Orsino.

ANTONIO   You do mistake me, sir.

1 OFFICER No, sir, no jot. I know your favour well,
 Though now you have no sea-cap on your head. 280
 Take him away; he knows I know him well.

ANTONIO I must obey. [*To Viola*] This comes with seeking you.
 But there's no remedy; I shall answer it.
 What will you do, now my necessity
 Makes me to ask you for my purse? It grieves me 285
 Much more for what I cannot do for you
 Than what befalls myself. You stand amazed,
 But be of comfort.

2 OFFICER Come, sir, away.

ANTONIO I must entreat of you some of that money. 290

VIOLA What money, sir?
 For the fair kindness you have showed me here,
 And part being prompted by your present trouble,
 Out of my lean and low ability
 I'll lend you something. My having is not much; 295
 I'll make division of my present with you.
 Hold, there's half my coffer.

ANTONIO Will you deny me now?
 Is't possible that my deserts to you
 Can lack persuasion? Do not tempt my misery, 300
 Lest that it make me so unsound a man
 As to upbraid you with those kindnesses
 That I have done for you.

VIOLA   I know of none,
 Nor know I you by voice or any feature.
 I hate ingratitude more in a man 305
 Than lying, vainness, babbling drunkenness,
 Or any taint of vice whose strong corruption
 Inhabits our frail blood.

Antonio reflects that good looks can hide bad character. He is led away to prison. Viola hopes that Antonio's mistake means that her brother is still alive. Sir Andrew vows to beat Viola. Sir Toby is unimpressed.

1 Putting Sebastian on a pedestal (in small groups)

Antonio has clearly put Sebastian on a pedestal, worshipping him like a god ('sanctity', 'image', 'venerable', 'devotion', 'idol', 'god'). Talk together about how Antonio's language adds to your impression of his friendship with Sebastian.

2 'In nature there's no blemish but the mind'

- Organise a class debate, using practical examples, on whether you agree with Antonio's words (line 318).
- Make a collage to illustrate lines 318–21 by collecting pictures of 'beauty' and 'evil', and intercutting them.
- Intercut lines 318–21 with Act 1 Scene 2, lines 48–51, and devise a dramatic presentation of the result.

3 Does Sir Toby overhear?

Sir Toby mocks rhyming couplets which express generalisations ('sage saws', lines 328–9). Identify the rhyming couplets in the script opposite. Do you think Sir Toby's sarcastic remark is prompted because he has overheard some or all of them?

4 They're all mad (in pairs)

Imagine the two officers consider each character in turn. Improvise or write their conversation as they wonder which ones are mad.

Relieved saved
sanctity holiness, sacredness
venerable worth deserving (of) devotion
trunks bodies
o'er-flourished overdressed
tane mistaken

sage saws wise sayings
Yet living in my glass is the mirror image of me
favour appearance, feature
Still always
paltry contemptible, mean
'Slid by God's eyelid

ANTONIO   O heavens themselves!

2 OFFICER Come, sir, I pray you go.

ANTONIO Let me speak a little. This youth that you see here,   310
    I snatched one-half out of the jaws of death,
    Relieved him with such sanctity of love;
    And to his image, which methought did promise
    Most venerable worth, did I devotion.

1 OFFICER What's that to us? The time goes by. Away!   315

ANTONIO But O how vile an idol proves this god!
    Thou hast, Sebastian, done good feature shame.
    In nature there's no blemish but the mind:
    None can be called deformed but the unkind.
    Virtue is beauty, but the beauteous-evil   320
    Are empty trunks, o'er-flourished by the devil.

1 OFFICER The man grows mad. Away with him! Come, come, sir.

ANTONIO Lead me on.

                            Exit [with Officers]

VIOLA Methinks his words do from such passion fly
    That he believes himself; so do not I.   325
    Prove true, imagination, O prove true,
    That I, dear brother, be now tane for you!

SIR TOBY Come hither, knight, come hither, Fabian. We'll whisper o'er
    a couplet or two of most sage saws.

VIOLA He named Sebastian. I my brother know   330
    Yet living in my glass; even such and so
    In favour was my brother, and he went
    Still in this fashion, colour, ornament,
    For him I imitate. O if it prove,
    Tempests are kind, and salt waves fresh in love.   *[Exit]*   335

SIR TOBY A very dishonest paltry boy, and more a coward than a hare;
    his dishonesty appears in leaving his friend here in necessity, and
    denying him; and for his cowardship, ask Fabian.

FABIAN A coward, a most devout coward, religious in it.

SIR ANDREW 'Slid, I'll after him again and beat him.   340

SIR TOBY Do, cuff him soundly, but never draw thy sword.

SIR ANDREW And I do not –   *[Exit]*

FABIAN Come, let's see the event.

SIR TOBY I dare lay any money, 'twill be nothing yet.

                            Exeunt

Looking back at Act 3
Activities for groups or individuals

1 Tourist guide of Illyria

In Scene 3, line 19 Sebastian sounds like a tourist: 'Shall we go see the relics of this town?'. Imagine that Illyria possesses a tourist office. What would its official guide say about the historic monuments of the town? Design a publicity leaflet for Illyria. Remember that in line 11 of Scene 3, Antonio says that Illyria can seem a 'rough and unhospitable place'. This means that there is something the tourist office would want to hide, or to describe euphemistically (using mild or vague expressions for harsh or blunt ones).

2 You can't hide your feelings

Olivia is convinced that love, like guilt, shows itself clearly in a person's face and behaviour. In Scene 1, line 133 she says: 'Love's night is noon' (love cannot be hidden).

Do you agree? Will love always show itself clearly? Using examples from your own experience, talk together about whether you think your deepest feelings can remain private to you and hidden from others.

3 Speaking to the audience

Viola, as Cesario, speaks many lines which are full of dramatic irony. The audience knows she is a woman, but everyone on stage thinks she is a man. Talk together about whether or not Viola should acknowledge the audience in any way when she speaks such lines. For example, in Scene 4, lines 255–6 she says: 'A little thing would make me tell them how much I lack of a man'. The lines usually raise a laugh, but do you think she should say them directly to the audience? Would it be out of character?

4 Where's Feste? (in small groups)

Why has Feste not yet been involved in the plot against Malvolio? Maria said she would involve him. Talk together about possible reasons for his absence.

Opponents in love. The duel brings together two lovers. Sir Andrew loves
Olivia, and thinks that Viola-Cesario is wooing her too. He does not suspect
that Viola-Cesario is a woman who loves Orsino! Make two lists. The first
identifies what Sir Andrew has in common with Viola, and the second list
sets out their differences.

Feste has mistaken Sebastian for Viola. Sebastian tries to get rid of him with money and a threat. Sir Andrew makes the same mistake, strikes Sebastian – and is hit in return!

1 'Nothing that is so is so' (in small groups)

'Feste's words are the motto of the play. They catch the essence of what *Twelfth Night* is about: that appearances are deceptive', wrote one student. Talk together about characters and actions you would select to justify (or to challenge) this student's claim.

2 From money, through beating, to romance

Scene 1 is filled with the consequences of mistaken identity. In turn, Feste, Sir Andrew, Sir Toby and Olivia mistake Sebastian for Viola. For that mistake:

> Feste receives money and the threat of a beating
> Sir Andrew gets a beating
> Sir Toby almost fights a duel
> Olivia seems about to get the man of her dreams.

Design a sequence of four pictures to show the consequences of mistaken identity in the scene.

3 Foolish Greek

In Shakespeare's day, 'Greek' (line 15) was used to describe unintelligible language. Even today English people say 'It's Greek to me' when they hear or read a language they don't understand. But why? Talk together about why you think Greek, rather than any other language or nation, should be stereotyped like this by English speakers.

Vent thy folly get rid of your foolishness
lubber awkward fool
cockney spoilt child, affected speaker
ungird thy strangeness stop pretending you don't know me

By my troth truly
open hand ready to give money (or to strike)
after fourteen years' purchase for a great deal of money (in Elizabethan England the price of land was equal to twelve years' rent)

ACT 4   SCENE I
The street outside Olivia's house

Enter SEBASTIAN *and* FESTE

FESTE Will you make me believe that I am not sent for you?

SEBASTIAN Go to, go to, thou art a foolish fellow.
      Let me be clear of thee.

FESTE Well held out, i'faith! No, I do not know you, nor I am not sent
to you by my lady to bid you come speak with her; nor your name   5
is not Master Cesario; nor this is not my nose neither. Nothing that
is so is so.

SEBASTIAN I prithee, vent thy folly somewhere else.
      Thou know'st not me.

FESTE Vent my folly! He has heard that word of some great man and   10
now applies it to a fool. Vent my folly! I am afraid this great lubber
the world will prove a cockney. I prithee now, ungird thy
strangeness and tell me what I shall vent to my lady. Shall I vent
to her that thou art coming?

SEBASTIAN I prithee, foolish Greek, depart from me.   15
      There's money for thee. If you tarry longer,
      I shall give worse payment.

FESTE By my troth, thou hast an open hand. These wise men that give
fools money get themselves a good report – after fourteen years'
purchase.   20

Enter [SIR] ANDREW, [SIR] TOBY, *and* FABIAN

SIR ANDREW Now, sir, have I met you again? There's for you!
      [*Strikes Sebastian*]

SEBASTIAN Why, there's for thee, and there, and there!
      [*Beats Sir Andrew*]
      Are all the people mad?

SIR TOBY Hold, sir, or I'll throw your dagger o'er the house.

Sir Toby challenges Sebastian to a fight, but Olivia intervenes and orders Sir Toby and his friends to leave. She invites Sebastian to go with her. He willingly agrees, wondering if it is all a dream.

1 Point of view

Consider the scene from Sebastian's point of view. First, he meets a Fool who calls him 'Cesario' and talks incomprehensibly about an invitation from a lady. Then he is assaulted by one man and threatened by another. Finally, a beautiful woman invites him lovingly into her house. No wonder he thinks he's either mad or dreaming – and wants to continue dreaming! ('Let fancy still . . . in Lethe steep' = let love always plunge my reason in the river of forgetfulness.)

- Write Sebastian's diary describing the events of the scene.
- Draw a graph, diagram or flow chart, plotting the events of the scene and changes of Sebastian's mood.

2 Typical language

Take each character in the scene in turn. Select one sentence, line or phrase which you think most accurately expresses their personality. Compare your choices with those of other students. Give your reasons for your own choice when you find differences of opinion.

3 What an entrance! What an invitation! (in pairs)

Olivia's lines 38–44 give every actor a tremendous opportunity to play the grand lady. Experiment with saying them to each other in the most powerful way you can. Add appropriate gestures. Remember, at this moment Olivia must totally command the stage!

Persuasion! Olivia has just saved the love of her life. Take turns to speak lines 44–58 in the most persuasive way you can. Speak each of her seven sentences in a different style.

---

action of battery summons for assault
put up your iron draw your sword
well fleshed experienced in bloodshed
malapert saucy
sway rule

uncivil and unjust extent boisterous and lawless assault
botched up clumsily carried out
Beshrew curse
He started . . . in thee he made my heart leap with fear
relish meaning

FESTE This will I tell my lady straight; I would not be in some of your   25
    coats for twopence.   [*Exit*]
SIR TOBY Come on, sir, hold!
SIR ANDREW Nay, let him alone. I'll go another way to work with him;
    I'll have an action of battery against him, if there be any law in
    Illyria. Though I struck him first, yet it's no matter for that.   30
SEBASTIAN Let go thy hand!
SIR TOBY Come, sir, I will not let you go. Come, my young soldier,
    put up your iron. You are well fleshed. Come on!
SEBASTIAN I will be free from thee. [*Draws his sword*] What wouldst
        thou now?
    If thou dar'st tempt me further, draw thy sword.   35
SIR TOBY What, what! Nay, then, I must have an ounce or two of this
    malapert blood from you. [*Draws*]

                    Enter OLIVIA

OLIVIA Hold, Toby! On thy life I charge thee hold!
SIR TOBY Madam –
OLIVIA Will it be ever thus? Ungracious wretch,   40
        Fit for the mountains and the barbarous caves,
        Where manners ne'er were preached! Out of my sight!
        Be not offended, dear Cesario.
        Rudesby, be gone!
                [*Exeunt Sir Toby, Sir Andrew, and Fabian*]
                        I prithee, gentle friend,
        Let thy fair wisdom, not thy passion, sway   45
        In this uncivil and unjust extent
        Against thy peace. Go with me to my house
        And hear thou there how many fruitless pranks
        This ruffian hath botched up, that thou thereby
        Mayst smile at this. Thou shalt not choose but go.   50
        Do not deny. Beshrew his soul for me,
        He started one poor heart of mine, in thee.
SEBASTIAN What relish is in this? How runs the stream?
        Or I am mad, or else this is a dream.
        Let fancy still my sense in Lethe steep;   55
        If it be thus to dream, still let me sleep!
OLIVIA Nay, come, I prithee; would thou'dst be ruled by me!
SEBASTIAN Madam, I will.
OLIVIA   O say so, and so be!
                                                            Exeunt

Maria encourages Feste to disguise himself as Sir Topas, the curate. He jokes with Sir Toby, then begins to torment the imprisoned Malvolio, treating Malvolio as if he were mad.

1 Jargon – making nonsense seem impressive

In Elizabethan times, priests like Sir Topas were often regarded as great scholars. But their learning became the subject of many jokes. Feste parodies the academic style of churchmen with his pretentious language and mock logic. He invents totally fictitious experts ('the old hermit of Prague') and imitates philosophical talk ('That that is, is'). In the previous scene, Feste said 'Nothing that is so is so'. Now he says just the opposite! It's all part of the topsy-turvy world of Illyria, where appearances are deceptive and all things are possible – or impossible!

- Speak lines 11–14 as if you were an old, learned professor, talking of very important truths. Practise until you have a version to share with the class.
- Invent another short speech for Feste in the same style of high-sounding nonsense in lines 11–14.

Shakespeare may also be making fun of the Church's claims to scholarship here, just as he does in lines 4–9: 'dissembled' (deceived), 'tall' (able to see over the pulpit), 'great scholar' (same as 'good housekeeper').

2 Setting the scene

Design a set for Scene 2. It should somehow include a 'dark room' where Malvolio is imprisoned, but must also allow the audience to understand just what's going on.

---

dissemble disguise, conceal my true identity
function role as priest
competitors conspirators
Bonos dies good day (bad Latin)

King Gorboduc legendary king of Britain
hyperbolical fantastical (exaggerated)
vexest thou you torment
use greet

ACT 4 SCENE 2
A room in Olivia's house

Enter MARIA *and* FESTE

MARIA Nay, I prithee put on this gown and this beard; make him believe thou art Sir Topas the curate. Do it quickly. I'll call Sir Toby the whilst.   *[Exit]*

FESTE Well, I'll put it on, and I will dissemble myself in't, and I would I were the first that ever dissembled in such a gown. I am not tall   5
enough to become the function well, nor lean enough to be thought a good student; but to be said an honest man and a good housekeeper goes as fairly as to say a careful man and a great scholar. The competitors enter.

Enter [SIR] TOBY [*and* MARIA]

SIR TOBY Jove bless thee, Master Parson.   10
FESTE *Bonos dies,* Sir Toby. For as the old hermit of Prague, that never saw pen and ink, very wittily said to a niece of King Gorboduc, 'That that is, is', so I, being Master Parson, am Master Parson; for what is 'that' but 'that' and 'is' but 'is'?
SIR TOBY To him, Sir Topas.   15
FESTE What ho, I say! Peace in this prison!
SIR TOBY The knave counterfeits well. A good knave.
MALVOLIO (*Within*) Who calls there?
FESTE Sir Topas the curate, who comes to visit Malvolio the lunatic.
MALVOLIO Sir Topas, Sir Topas, good Sir Topas, go to my lady.   20
FESTE Out, hyperbolical fiend! How vexest thou this man! Talk'st thou nothing but of ladies?
SIR TOBY Well said, Master Parson.
MALVOLIO Sir Topas, never was man thus wronged. Good Sir Topas, do not think I am mad. They have laid me here in hideous darkness.   25
FESTE Fie, thou dishonest Satan! I call thee by the most modest terms, for I am one of those gentle ones that will use the devil himself with courtesy. Say'st thou that the house is dark?
MALVOLIO As hell, Sir Topas.

Malvolio protests that he is not mad, and that his prison is too dark. Feste (as Sir Topas) refuses to believe him and continues to torment him. Sir Toby wishes the whole business was over.

1 Catch 22: a no-win situation (in pairs)

Whatever Malvolio says, he cannot win, because Feste is determined to treat all his remarks as if they were made by a madman. Feste's strategy is clear: he will torment Malvolio by turning logic on its head to increase Malvolio's confusion and frustration. For example, he says that 'barricadoes' (fortifications) and 'ebony' (black wood) are 'transparent' and 'lustrous' (bright).

'The Egyptians in their fog' Feste refers to one of the plagues which Moses brought down upon Egypt in the Bible (Exodus, chapter 10): God caused 'thick darkness for three days'.

Pythagoras The Greek philosopher and mathematician, who is known today for his theorem about right-angled triangles. But in Shakespeare's time he was known for his doctrine of the transmigration of souls: that when a person died, his or her soul migrated to another human or animal body. This doctrine of reincarnation is rejected by Christian teaching which believes in the resurrection of the body. As a devout puritan, Malvolio would find Pythagoras' notion very offensive.

Take parts as Feste and Malvolio. Read lines 20–48. Feste should be as rational as possible. Swap roles and read again. Then talk together about whether you feel sympathy for Malvolio. Do you think Feste's humour is genuinely funny, or is it bitter and vicious?

---

clerestories windows in the upper part of a wall
constant normal
grandam grandmother
haply perhaps
allow of thy wits certify you are sane

I am for all waters I can do anything
knavery trickery
upshot finish
perdy by God (*par Dieu*)

FESTE Why, it hath bay windows transparent as barricadoes, and the   30
    clerestories toward the south-north are as lustrous as ebony; and
    yet complain'st thou of obstruction?

MALVOLIO I am not mad, Sir Topas; I say to you this house is dark.

FESTE Madman, thou errest. I say there is no darkness but ignorance,
    in which thou art more puzzled than the Egyptians in their fog.   35

MALVOLIO I say this house is as dark as ignorance, though ignorance
    were as dark as hell; and I say there was never man thus abused.
    I am no more mad than you are. Make the trial of it in any constant
    question.

FESTE What is the opinion of Pythagoras concerning wildfowl?   40

MALVOLIO That the soul of our grandam might haply inhabit a bird.

FESTE What think'st thou of his opinion?

MALVOLIO I think nobly of the soul, and no way approve his opinion.

FESTE Fare thee well. Remain thou still in darkness. Thou shalt hold
    th'opinion of Pythagoras ere I will allow of thy wits, and fear to   45
    kill a woodcock lest thou dispossess the soul of thy grandam. Fare
    thee well.

MALVOLIO Sir Topas, Sir Topas!

SIR TOBY My most exquisite Sir Topas!

FESTE Nay, I am for all waters.   50

MARIA Thou mightst have done this without thy beard and gown; he
    sees thee not.

SIR TOBY To him in thine own voice, and bring me word how thou
    find'st him. I would we were well rid of this knavery. If he may
    be conveniently delivered, I would he were, for I am now so far   55
    in offence with my niece that I cannot pursue with any safety this
    sport to the upshot. [*To Maria*] Come by and by to my chamber.
                                   Exit [with Maria]

FESTE [*Sings*]   Hey Robin, jolly Robin,
                  Tell me how thy lady does.

MALVOLIO Fool!   60

FESTE [*Sings*]   My lady is unkind, perdy.

MALVOLIO Fool!

FESTE [*Sings*]   Alas, why is she so?

MALVOLIO Fool, I say!

FESTE [*Sings*]   She loves another –   65
    Who calls, ha?

Malvolio begs Feste for pen and paper to write a letter to Olivia. Feste continues to torment him by pretending to have a conversation with Sir Topas. Feste agrees to help the 'mad' Malvolio.

Malvolio and Sir Topas. Shakespeare Memorial Theatre, 1955.

propertied me treated me as an object, not a human being
face me out of my wits make me think I'm mad
Advise you be careful

God b'w'you God be with you
shent scolded
advantage profit
bearing delivering, carrying
counterfeit pretend

MALVOLIO Good fool, as ever thou wilt deserve well at my hand, help
me to a candle and pen, ink, and paper. As I am a gentleman, I
will live to be thankful to thee for't.

FESTE Master Malvolio?   70

MALVOLIO Ay, good fool.

FESTE Alas, sir, how fell you besides your five wits?

MALVOLIO Fool, there was never man so notoriously abused. I am as
well in my wits, fool, as thou art.

FESTE But as well? Then you are mad indeed, if you be no better in   75
your wits than a fool.

MALVOLIO They have here propertied me: keep me in darkness, send
ministers to me, asses, and do all they can to face me out of my
wits.

FESTE Advise you what you say. The minister is here. [*As Sir Topas*]   80
Malvolio, Malvolio, thy wits the heavens restore. Endeavour thyself
to sleep and leave thy vain bibble babble.

MALVOLIO Sir Topas!

FESTE [*As Sir Topas*] Maintain no words with him, good fellow. [*As
himself*] Who, I, sir? Not I, sir. God b'w'you, good Sir Topas.   85
[*As Sir Topas*] Marry, amen. [*As himself*] I will, sir, I will.

MALVOLIO Fool, fool, fool, I say!

FESTE Alas, sir, be patient. What say you, sir? I am shent for speaking
to you.

MALVOLIO Good fool, help me to some light and some paper; I tell   90
thee, I am as well in my wits as any man in Illyria.

FESTE Well-a-day, that you were, sir!

MALVOLIO By this hand, I am! Good fool, some ink, paper and light,
and convey what I will set down to my lady. It shall advantage thee
more than ever the bearing of letter did.   95

FESTE I will help you to't. But tell me true, are you not mad indeed
or do you but counterfeit?

MALVOLIO Believe me, I am not. I tell thee true.

FESTE Nay, I'll ne'er believe a madman till I see his brains. I will fetch
you light and paper and ink.   100

Malvolio promises to reward Feste who, with a song, leaves to fetch pen and paper. In Scene 3, Sebastian reflects on his good fortune. He wonders what has happened to Antonio, whose advice he needs.

1 Feste's song (in small groups)

- Compose an appropriate tune for Feste's song.
- Fit actions to each line.
- Is Feste's last line ('Adieu, goodman devil') spoken to Malvolio? Or is it simply part of Vice's talk with the devil? Advise the actor.

2 A change of scene

Scene 3 changes from the tormenting of Malvolio to Sebastian wondering about the strange events that have happened to him.

a How would you manage the scene change so that the action flows easily between Feste's exit and Sebastian's entrance?

b Identify several ways in which the two scenes echo each other. Lines 1–4 will help you.

3 Sebastian's soliloquy (in pairs)

Talk together about whether Sebastian should speak some, none, or all of his lines 1–21 to the audience or to himself. Write a set of notes for the lines. They should aim to help the actor to bring out all the comedy he can from Sebastian's wonderment.

requite reward
old Vice a character in medieval plays (who cut the devil's nails with a wooden dagger)

lath wood
Pare cut
there he was he had been there
credit news, report

MALVOLIO Fool, I'll requite it in the highest degree. I prithee be gone.

FESTE [*Sings*]   I am gone, sir,
And anon, sir,
   I'll be with you again,
In a trice   105
Like to the old Vice,
   Your need to sustain;
Who, with dagger of lath,
In his rage and his wrath,
   Cries, 'Ah ha' to the devil,   110
Like a mad lad,
'Pare thy nails, dad?'
   Adieu, goodman devil.   *Exit*

ACT 4   SCENE 3
In Olivia's garden

Enter SEBASTIAN

SEBASTIAN This is the air, that is the glorious sun,
This pearl she gave me, I do feel't and see't,
And though 'tis wonder that enwraps me thus,
Yet 'tis not madness. Where's Antonio then?
I could not find him at the Elephant,   5
Yet there he was, and there I found this credit,
That he did range the town to seek me out.
His counsel now might do me golden service,

Sebastian decides that Olivia cannot be mad, because she rules her household with total competence. Olivia arrives with a priest and proposes instant marriage. Sebastian agrees.

1 A secret marriage (in small groups)

Olivia proposes an instant marriage, but promises it will be kept secret until Sebastian is willing to make it public. Then, they will have a grand ceremony ('celebration'), suitable for her high social status ('birth'). Talk together about the following questions:

a Why does Olivia want a secret marriage?
b What does the silent priest make of it all?
c What's happened to her vow to mourn her brother for seven years?
d Why hasn't she called Sebastian 'Cesario' and so discovered her mistake?
e What do you think is the dramatic purpose of this scene?
f Have you ever heard of anybody who got married very quickly when he or she was abroad in a strange place?
g Should you just forget all the puzzles of a–f above and simply enjoy the unlikely events that Shakespeare piles up?

2 What does Sebastian think? (in pairs)

Try these two activities to see if you can get inside Sebastian's mind:

● One person speaks Olivia's lines 22–31, pausing at each punctuation mark. In each pause, the other person says 'that I am mad, or else the lady's mad'.
● Repeat the activity, but this time, in each pause, Sebastian reveals his secret thoughts about what Olivia has just said.

3 Your view of Olivia?

What does line 27 add to your view of Olivia's personality?

---

disputes well agrees
instance example
discourse reason
sway rule
dispatch carry out
deceivable misleading

chantry by nearby chapel
Plight pledge
Whiles until
come to note become known
fairly note bless

For though my soul disputes well with my sense
That this may be some error, but no madness,   10
Yet doth this accident and flood of fortune
So far exceed all instance, all discourse,
That I am ready to distrust mine eyes,
And wrangle with my reason that persuades me
To any other trust but that I am mad,   15
Or else the lady's mad; yet if 'twere so,
She could not sway her house, command her followers,
Take and give back affairs and them dispatch,
With such a smooth, discreet, and stable bearing
As I perceive she does. There's something in't   20
That is deceivable. But here the lady comes.

Enter OLIVIA *and* PRIEST

OLIVIA Blame not this haste of mine. If you mean well,
Now go with me, and with this holy man
Into the chantry by; there before him,
And underneath that consecrated roof,   25
Plight me the full assurance of your faith,
That my most jealous and too doubtful soul
May live at peace. He shall conceal it
Whiles you are willing it shall come to note;
What time we will our celebration keep   30
According to my birth. What do you say?
SEBASTIAN I'll follow this good man, and go with you,
And having sworn truth, ever will be true.
OLIVIA Then lead the way, good father, and heavens so shine,
That they may fairly note this act of mine!   35
                                                        Exeunt

Looking back at Act 4
Activities for groups or individuals

1 Mistaken identity

In Scene 1, Feste, Sir Andrew and Olivia all mistake Sebastian for Viola. What would happen if you were constantly being mistaken for someone who is your double? Improvise a sequence in which you are mistaken for someone else.

2 True lover, or . . . ?

Has Sebastian fallen in love with Olivia? Or is he just taking advantage of her money and status? Think about your view of his character and try to guess at his true feelings as Olivia leads him off to marriage at the end of Act 4.

3 What's in a name?

Here are some suggestions about the characters' names:

> *Orsino* little bear? (Italian), musical? ('ostinato' = a repeated musical phrase).
> *Feste* festive? quick? (from 'festinare' in Latin).
> *Sir Toby Belch* coarse, earthy, crude?
> *Sir Andrew Aguecheek* sickly face?
> *Viola* a musical name? almost an anagram of Olivia?
> *Malvolio* evil wishing (from 'male volente' in Latin)?
> *Sir Topas* topaz (a precious stone, thought to cure madness)? or from *The Tale of Sir Topas*, a story by Chaucer about a ridiculous knight.

Talk together about whether you think the characters' names are a true indication of their personalities. Do you have any other ideas about their possible meaning or significance?

4 Revenge is sweet?

a Does Feste really enjoy his opportunity for revenge?
b Do you think that Feste teases or torments Malvolio?
c Does Malvolio deserve what he gets?
d What is your own attitude to what happens to Malvolio in Scene 3?

Malvolio's progress. This is how four different productions have presented
Malvolio at particular points in the play. Look back through the first four
acts to identify which moment you think each picture represents. Choose
suitable captions from the script.

Feste will not let Fabian see Malvolio's letter. He entertains Orsino with his word-juggling, and encourages him to hand over more money.

---

1 Comedian and stooge? (in groups of three)

Feste treats both Fabian and Orsino as the 'stooge' or 'straight man', the partner who feeds lines to a comedian, so that the comedian can make a witty point. Practise reading lines 1–38 with Feste as a kind of music-hall comedian, scoring points off his partner. Then try other styles of speaking. Which do you think is most appropriate for Feste?

2 Explaining the joke

Explaining a joke is a sure way to kill the humour. But two things Feste says would have made his Elizabethan audience laugh because they were well known at the time:

line 5 Queen Elizabeth I begged a dog from a courtier saying she would grant any request in return. He replied 'Give me my dog again'.

lines 16–17 A favourite joke among men of the time was that a girl's 'no, no, no, no' actually meant 'yes, yes'. Can you work out how four negatives make two affirmatives? Another explanation is that negatives meant 'lips' and affirmatives meant 'mouths'. So four lips made two mouths.

3 Mocking Orsino?

Orsino is the most powerful person in Illyria, but Feste is almost rude to him. Try reading lines 6–38 so that Feste mocks Orsino, coming extremely close to being disrespectful to him. How does Orsino speak his lines if Feste is almost openly cheeky? Experiment with ways of showing that Orsino half suspects that he is being mocked, and becomes increasingly irritated about it.

---

trappings hangers-on, adornments
By my troth by my faith (truthfully)
double-dealing deception (or giving twice)

grace honour
flesh and blood human nature (as opposed to 'grace')

ACT 5 SCENE 1
In Olivia's garden

Enter FESTE *and* FABIAN

FABIAN Now, as thou lov'st me, let me see his letter.

FESTE Good Master Fabian, grant me another request.

FABIAN Anything.

FESTE Do not desire to see this letter.

FABIAN This is to give a dog and in recompense desire my dog again. 5

ORSINO Belong you to the Lady Olivia, friends?

FESTE Ay, sir, we are some of her trappings.

ORSINO I know thee well. How dost thou, my good fellow?

FESTE Truly, sir, the better for my foes, and the worse for my friends.

ORSINO Just the contrary: the better for thy friends. 10

FESTE No, sir, the worse.

ORSINO How can that be?

FESTE Marry, sir, they praise me, and make an ass of me. Now my foes
tell me plainly I am an ass, so that by my foes, sir, I profit in the
knowledge of myself, and by my friends I am abused; so that, 15
conclusions to be as kisses, if your four negatives make your two
affirmatives, why then, the worse for my friends and the better for
my foes.

ORSINO Why, this is excellent.

FESTE By my troth, sir, no, though it please you to be one of my friends. 20

ORSINO Thou shalt not be the worse for me; there's gold.

FESTE But that it would be double-dealing, sir, I would you could make
it another.

ORSINO O you give me ill counsel.

FESTE Put your grace in your pocket, sir, for this once, and let your 25
flesh and blood obey it.

Feste tries to persuade Orsino to give him more money, but is sent to fetch Olivia. The officers bring Antonio. He is recognised by Orsino as a past enemy, and by Viola as the one who rescued her in the duel.

1 Third time lucky?

Feste tries to beg a third coin from Orsino by using Latin (*'Primo, secundo, tertio'* = one, two, three), dance music ('measure' = dance) and church bells (St Bennet was a London church). Feste says he's not greedy for money, but clearly hopes that bringing Olivia will result in a further reward from Orsino. Why do you think Feste is so keen to get money out of Orsino? Is it his personality, or is it part of his job as a professional Fool?

2 Sea-battle!

Antonio obviously did great deeds in a destructive fight ('scathful grapple') against Orsino's fleet. His own ship was tiny and hardly worth capturing ('baubling . . . shallow draught and bulk unprizable'). But he outfought Orsino's best ship ('most noble bottom'), and captured another with all her cargo from Crete ('the Phoenix and her fraught from Candy'). His bravery made his Illyrian enemies admire him, even though he inflicted such terrible losses on them.

Write the report of the sea-battle (based on lines 40–52) from the viewpoint of one or more of the following: Antonio, Titus, Orsino, the Captain of the Phoenix or the Tiger, or an ordinary seaman.

3 The voice of authority (in pairs)

Orsino is the military commander as well as ruler of Illyria. All his previous appearances have been concerned with love, but now he takes on his official duties and speaks as a leader. Experiment with different styles of speaking the lines Orsino says to Antonio. Decide how you think Orsino should speak to Antonio.

---

triplex triple time in music
bounty generosity
covetousness ardent desire for money
Vulcan Roman god of fire, blacksmith to the gods (see page 165)

desp'rate of shame and state recklessly disregarding disgrace and danger
distraction madness
Notable notorious
dear costly, grievous

ORSINO   Well, I will be so much a sinner to be a double-dealer; there's
    another.
FESTE   *Primo, secundo, tertio* is a good play, and the old saying is 'The
    third pays for all'; the triplex, sir, is a good tripping measure; or   30
    the bells of St Bennet, sir, may put you in mind - one, two, three.
ORSINO   You can fool no more money out of me at this throw. If you
    will let your lady know I am here to speak with her, and bring her
    along with you, it may awake my bounty further.
FESTE   Marry, sir, lullaby to your bounty till I come again. I go, sir,   35
    but I would not have you to think that my desire of having is the
    sin of covetousness; but, as you say, sir, let your bounty take a nap.
    I will awake it anon.   *Exit*

            Enter ANTONIO *and* OFFICERS

VIOLA   Here comes the man, sir, that did rescue me.
ORSINO   That face of his I do remember well;   40
            Yet when I saw it last, it was besmeared
            As black as Vulcan, in the smoke of war.
            A baubling vessel was he captain of,
            For shallow draught and bulk unprizable,
            With which, such scathful grapple did he make   45
            With the most noble bottom of our fleet,
            That very envy, and the tongue of loss,
            Cried fame and honour on him. What's the matter?
1 OFFICER   Orsino, this is that Antonio
            That took the Phoenix and her fraught from Candy,   50
            And this is he that did the Tiger board,
            When your young nephew Titus lost his leg.
            Here in the streets, desp'rate of shame and state,
            In private brabble did we apprehend him.
VIOLA   He did me kindness, sir, drew on my side,   55
            But in conclusion put strange speech upon me,
            I know not what 'twas, but distraction.
ORSINO   Notable pirate! Thou salt-water thief!
            What foolish boldness brought thee to their mercies,
            Whom thou, in terms so bloody and so dear,   60
            Hast made thine enemies?

Antonio tells the story of how he rescued Sebastian, protected him and lent him money. Orsino dismisses the explanation as madness. Olivia arrives and mistakes Viola for Sebastian.

1 Antonio's story (in small groups)

Lines 66–81 tell the story of Antonio and Sebastian, and the mistaking of Viola. Identify as many actions as you can and show them as a mime whilst one person narrates. You'll find it good fun (and helpful to your understanding) if you play a 'fast-forward' version after your prepared version.

2 'A twenty-years' removèd thing' (in pairs)

Prepare two tableaux, 'before' and 'after'. The first tableau shows warm friendship, the second shows what happens after twenty years' separation. Compare your version with those of other pairs.

3 Three months or a few days?

Theatre audiences rarely notice that Shakespeare seems to have forgotten what he wrote earlier in the play. Both Antonio and Orsino say that three months have passed since Viola came to court. But in Act 1 Scene 4, lines 2–3, Valentine says: 'he hath known you but three days'.

Imagine you are a teacher or lecturer. One of your students asks you if Shakespeare made a mistake. What do you reply?

4 First meeting

This is the first time that Orsino and Olivia meet in the play. Advise the actors how they can make the most of the stage direction: '*Enter* OLIVIA *and Attendants*', Orsino's line 86, and Olivia's lines 90–2.

---

base and ground firm reason
wrack wreckage
beset attacked
partake share
face . . . aquaintance deny he knew me

int'rim interim, time between
vacancy absence
tended upon served (attended)
anon soon
serviceable of help

ANTONIO   Orsino, noble sir,
            Be pleased that I shake off these names you give me.
            Antonio never yet was thief or pirate,
            Though I confess, on base and ground enough,
            Orsino's enemy. A witchcraft drew me hither   65
            That most ungrateful boy there by your side,
            From the rude sea's enraged and foamy mouth
            Did I redeem; a wrack past hope he was.
            His life I gave him, and did thereto add
            My love without retention, or restraint,   70
            All his in dedication. For his sake,
            Did I expose myself, pure for his love,
            Into the danger of this adverse town,
            Drew to defend him when he was beset;
            Where being apprehended, his false cunning   75
            (Not meaning to partake with me in danger)
            Taught him to face me out of his acquaintance,
            And grew a twenty-years' removèd thing
            While one would wink; denied me mine own purse,
            Which I had recommended to his use   80
            Not half an hour before.
VIOLA   How can this be?
ORSINO When came he to this town?
ANTONIO Today, my lord, and for three months before,
            No int'rim, not a minute's vacancy,
            Both day and night did we keep company.   85

                    Enter OLIVIA *and Attendants*

ORSINO Here comes the countess; now heaven walks on earth.
            But for thee, fellow – Fellow, thy words are madness.
            Three months this youth hath tended upon me,
            But more of that anon. Take him aside.
OLIVIA What would my lord, but that he may not have,   90
            Wherein Olivia may seem serviceable?
            Cesario, you do not keep promise with me.
VIOLA Madam!
ORSINO Gracious Olivia –
OLIVIA What do you say, Cesario? Good my lord –   95

Olivia again rejects Orsino's love. He threatens to kill Viola-Cesario because he suspects that Olivia loves 'him'. Viola-Cesario willingly agrees to go with Orsino. Olivia feels that she has been deceived. She sends for the Priest.

1 Speaking the lines

Actors often disagree about how Orsino should speak his reply to Olivia in lines 101–4. Does he snap the lines at her? Or does he try to win her sympathy? How does he speak the four words 'What shall I do?'

How does Olivia reply in line 105: off-handedly? challengingly? sharply? coldly? dismissively? sympathetically ('shall become' = that brings honour to)?

Explore ways of speaking the lines. Try varying the mood for each sentence. Which way do you feel is the most appropriate?

2 Love or cruelty? (in pairs)

After all his religious language in lines 102–4 ('altars', 'soul', 'faithfull'st', 'devotion'), Orsino suddenly turns cruel and threatens to kill Viola-Cesario to spite Olivia. To help you decide whether or not he would really carry out his threat, speak lines 106–20:

- as a dangerous threat, meaning it
- as a hopeless plea, not meaning it
- speaking only one or two key words in each line.

3 The Egyptian thief

Thyamus, a legendary Egyptian thief, was surrounded by his enemies. He attempted to kill the woman he loved, so that she would not fall into their hands. Was that love?

---

aught anything
fat and fulsome gross and distasteful
ingrate ungrateful
unauspicious ill-omened
savours nobly tastes honourable
cast throw aside
screws me from forces me out of

marble-breasted hard-hearted
minion favourite
tender esteem, hold, regard
jocund gladly
do you rest give you comfort
feign pretend
beguiled deceived

VIOLA My lord would speak; my duty hushes me.

OLIVIA If it be aught to the old tune, my lord,
    It is as fat and fulsome to mine ear
    As howling after music.

ORSINO   Still so cruel?

OLIVIA Still so constant, lord.   100

ORSINO What, to perverseness? You uncivil lady,
    To whose ingrate and unauspicious altars
    My soul the faithfull'st off'rings have breathed out
    That e'er devotion tendered! What shall I do?

OLIVIA Even what it please my lord that shall become him.   105

ORSINO Why should I not – had I the heart to do it –
    Like to th'Egyptian thief at point of death
    Kill what I love – a savage jealousy
    That sometimes savours nobly? But hear me this.
    Since you to non-regardance cast my faith,   110
    And that I partly know the instrument
    That screws me from my true place in your favour,
    Live you the marble-breasted tyrant still.
    But this your minion, whom I know you love,
    And whom, by heaven I swear, I tender dearly,   115
    Him will I tear out of that cruel eye
    Where he sits crownèd in his master's spite.
    Come, boy, with me; my thoughts are ripe in mischief.
    I'll sacrifice the lamb that I do love,
    To spite a raven's heart within a dove. [*Leaving*]   120

VIOLA And I most jocund, apt, and willingly,
    To do you rest, a thousand deaths would die. [*Following*]

OLIVIA Where goes Cesario?

VIOLA   After him I love
    More than I love these eyes, more than my life,
    More, by all mores, than e'er I shall love wife.   125
    If I do feign, you witnesses above
    Punish my life for tainting of my love!

OLIVIA Ay me, detested! How am I beguiled!

VIOLA Who does beguile you? Who does do you wrong?

OLIVIA Hast thou forgot thyself? Is it so long?   130
    Call forth the holy father.

                     [*Exit an Attendant*]

Olivia claims Viola-Cesario as her husband, mistaking 'him' for Sebastian. The Priest confirms the marriage. Orsino scolds Viola-Cesario for lying.

---

1 'Husband?'

Every director of *Twelfth Night* seizes the opportunity to make Orsino's 'Husband?' (line 133) a memorable moment. Everyone freezes as they take in the significance of what's happened. Make up a sentence for each character on stage to show what's in their mind at this moment.

2 Appearance = reality?

At line 138, Olivia challenges the play's theme of false identity: 'Be that thou know'st thou art' (admit what you truly are, namely my husband). But her appeal is full of unconscious irony, and actually reinforces the notion that things in Illyria are never what they seem. Why?

3 The Priest (in pairs)

Find a way of speaking the Priest's lines 145–52 which challenges the stereotype of stage priests as silly-voiced comics.

4 Language change – grizzle

Today, most people probably interpret Orsino's harsh words to Viola-Cesario 'What wilt thou be/When time hath sowed a grizzle on thy case?' as 'what are you going to be like when you've become discontented and grumbling (grizzly)'. But in Shakespeare's day, 'grizzle' meant 'grey hairs'.

---

strangle thy propriety deny your identity (as husband)
'tis ripe the proper time
mutual joinder agreed joining
compact contract of marriage

function job as a priest
dissembling deceitful
case body, skin
trip stumble (or trap)

ORSINO   Come, away!
OLIVIA Whither, my lord? Cesario, husband, stay!
ORSINO Husband?
OLIVIA   Ay, husband. Can he that deny?
ORSINO Her husband, sirrah?
VIOLA   No, my lord, not I.
OLIVIA Alas, it is the baseness of thy fear   135
      That makes thee strangle thy propriety.
      Fear not, Cesario, take thy fortunes up;
      Be that thou know'st thou art, and then thou art
      As great as that thou fear'st.

              Enter PRIEST

                  O welcome, father!
      Father, I charge thee by thy reverence   140
      Here to unfold – though lately we intended
      To keep in darkness what occasion now
      Reveals before 'tis ripe – what thou dost know
      Hath newly passed between this youth and me.
PRIEST A contract of eternal bond of love,   145
      Confirmed by mutual joinder of your hands,
      Attested by the holy close of lips,
      Strengthened by th'interchangement of your rings,
      And all the ceremony of this compact
      Sealed in my function, by my testimony;   150
      Since when, my watch hath told me, toward my grave
      I have travelled but two hours.
ORSINO [*To Viola*] O thou dissembling cub! What wilt thou be
      When time hath sowed a grizzle on thy case?
      Or will not else thy craft so quickly grow   155
      That thine own trip shall be thine overthrow?
      Farewell, and take her, but direct thy feet
      Where thou and I henceforth may never meet.
VIOLA My lord, I do protest –
OLIVIA   O do not swear!
      Hold little faith, though thou hast too much fear.   160

Sir Andrew complains he has been wounded by Viola-Cesario. Viola-Cesario denies doing it. Sir Toby enters – he has also been attacked. He scornfully dismisses Sir Andrew's offer of help.

1 True colours

Sir Toby contemptuously rejects Sir Andrew's friendship. In lines 190–1, Sir Toby shows what he really thinks of Sir Andrew: 'an ass-head, and a coxcomb (conceited fool), and a knave, a thin-faced knave, a gull'.

This is the final appearance of Sir Andrew and Sir Toby. The two actors will want to make as strong an impression as possible on the audience. Work out how you would present the stage direction *'Exeunt Feste, Fabian, Sir Toby and Sir Andrew'*. Your version should bring out each man's character clearly. Remember that action and gesture can emphasise or change the force of Sir Toby's words. Would you, as a director, want the audience to sympathise with or dislike each of these four characters?

2 'Passy-measures pavin'

No one can be quite sure what Sir Toby means in line 185. Possibly the best guess is 'drunken slowcoach', because Sir Toby drunkenly slurs 'passing measure pavane' (a slow and stately dance). Make up your own suggestion of what is in Sir Toby's mind.

---

presently immediately
bloody coxcomb bleeding head
incardinate incarnate (in the flesh)
'Od's lifelings by God's life
bespake you fair spoke kindly to you
halting limping

othergates in another way, otherwise
Sot drunkard (or fool)
his eyes were set blind drunk
dressed bandaged
gull fool, dupe

Enter SIR ANDREW [*his head bleeding*]

SIR ANDREW For the love of God, a surgeon! Send one presently to
Sir Toby.

OLIVIA What's the matter?

SIR ANDREW H'as broke my head across, and has given Sir Toby a
bloody coxcomb, too. For the love of God, your help! I had rather   165
than forty pound I were at home.

OLIVIA Who has done this, Sir Andrew?

SIR ANDREW The count's gentleman, one Cesario. We took him for a
coward, but he's the very devil incardinate.

ORSINO My gentleman Cesario?   170

SIR ANDREW 'Od's lifelings, here he is! You broke my head for nothing,
and that that I did, I was set on to do't by Sir Toby.

VIOLA Why do you speak to me? I never hurt you.
You drew your sword upon me without cause,
But I bespake you fair, and hurt you not.   175

Enter [SIR] TOBY *and* CLOWN [FESTE]

SIR ANDREW If a bloody coxcomb be a hurt, you have hurt me; I think
you set nothing by a bloody coxcomb. Here comes Sir Toby
halting – you shall hear more; but if he had not been in drink, he
would have tickled you othergates than he did.

ORSINO How now, gentleman? How is't with you?   180

SIR TOBY That's all one. H'as hurt me, and there's th'end on't. Sot,
didst see Dick Surgeon, sot?

FESTE O he's drunk, Sir Toby, an hour agone; his eyes were set at eight
i'th'morning.

SIR TOBY Then he's a rogue, and a passy-measures pavin. I hate a   185
drunken rogue.

OLIVIA Away with him! Who hath made this havoc with them?

SIR ANDREW I'll help you, Sir Toby, because we'll be dressed
together.

SIR TOBY Will you help – an ass-head, and a coxcomb, and a knave,   190
a thin-faced knave, a gull?

OLIVIA Get him to bed, and let his hurt be looked to.
[*Exeunt Feste, Fabian, Sir Toby, and Sir Andrew*]

Sebastian's appearance amazes everyone. Antonio expresses everyone's thoughts on seeing a double vision. The twins question each other and begin to find out that they are indeed related.

'An apple cleft in two is not more twin.' Everyone is amazed to see two Cesarios. How can one person be in two places at once? No one believes the evidence of their own eyes. Orsino calls it 'A natural perspective' (a distorting mirror which makes one image into two). But how closely should the actors playing Viola and Sebastian resemble each other? Design their costumes and suggest which hair-style and mannerisms the twins would have.

strange regard odd look
but so late ago not long ago
habit costume
racked pained
deity divinity (like God, everywhere at the same time)

suited dressed like that
in that dimension . . . participate still the same person as I was born
as the rest goes even as everything else suggests

Enter SEBASTIAN

SEBASTIAN I am sorry, madam, I have hurt your kinsman.
　　　　　But had it been the brother of my blood,
　　　　　I must have done no less with wit and safety.　　195
　　　　　You throw a strange regard upon me, and by that
　　　　　I do perceive it hath offended you.
　　　　　Pardon me, sweet one, even for the vows
　　　　　We made each other but so late ago.
ORSINO One face, one voice, one habit, and two persons –　　200
　　　　　A natural perspective, that is and is not!
SEBASTIAN Antonio! O my dear Antonio,
　　　　　How have the hours racked and tortured me,
　　　　　Since I have lost thee!
ANTONIO Sebastian are you?
SEBASTIAN　　　　　　　　Fear'st thou that, Antonio?　　205
ANTONIO How have you made division of yourself?
　　　　　An apple cleft in two is not more twin
　　　　　Than these two creatures. Which is Sebastian?
OLIVIA Most wonderful!
SEBASTIAN Do I stand there? I never had a brother;　　210
　　　　　Nor can there be that deity in my nature
　　　　　Of here and everywhere. I had a sister,
　　　　　Whom the blind waves and surges have devoured.
　　　　　Of charity, what kin are you to me?
　　　　　What countryman? What name? What parentage?　　215
VIOLA Of Messaline. Sebastian was my father;
　　　　　Such a Sebastian was my brother, too;
　　　　　So went he suited to his wat'ry tomb.
　　　　　If spirits can assume both form and suit,
　　　　　You come to fright us.
SEBASTIAN　　　　　　　　A spirit I am indeed,　　220
　　　　　But am in that dimension grossly clad
　　　　　Which from the womb I did participate.
　　　　　Were you a woman – as the rest goes even –
　　　　　I should my tears let fall upon your cheek,
　　　　　And say, 'Thrice welcome, drownèd Viola.'　　225

All is revealed! Sebastian and Viola are reunited. Viola tells of her disguise. Orsino hints at marriage. Viola confirms that she loves him. She reports that Malvolio has had the Captain arrested.

1 A tender reunion (in small groups)

The twins' reunion can be a moving theatrical experience. Every director must consider how to play certain moments on stage. Talk together about the following:

a Why do you think Viola forbids an embrace at line 235?
b What would be the effect if they did embrace at that point?
c How should Viola say line 242: coyly? laughingly? in an embarrassed way? or in some other way? How does everyone on stage react to Viola's line?
d How delicately should Sebastian say line 243?

2 Nature sorts things out!

Sebastian tells Olivia that she could have been engaged to a woman, 'But nature to her bias drew in that' (line 244). The image is from the game of bowls. Because each bowl has a lead weight (a bias) inside, it does not run straight, but runs towards its target along an indirect, curved route. So Sebastian suggests that eventually, if somewhat indirectly, nature sorts out muddles and mistakes as it follows its course. Suggest an action that Sebastian could perform as he speaks line 244, to make his meaning clear to the audience.

3 Orsino's love

Orsino suddenly switches his love from Olivia to Viola (line 250) when he discovers that his handsome page is really a woman. As director of the play, would you want to make the audience laugh at this sudden switch of affection? Or would you try to produce some other response?

---

lets hinders, interferes
usurped falsely taken
cohere and jump concur and agree
maiden weeds women's clothes
occurrence of my fortune
  happenings of my life
contracted betrothed, engaged

glass mirror (the perspective of line
  201 is truthful)
happy wreck fortunate accident
orbèd continent sun
action lawsuit
in durance imprisoned
suit legal action

VIOLA My father had a mole upon his brow.

SEBASTIAN And so had mine.

VIOLA And died that day when Viola from her birth
      Had numbered thirteen years.

SEBASTIAN O that record is lively in my soul! 230
      He finished indeed his mortal act
      That day that made my sister thirteen years.

VIOLA If nothing lets to make us happy both,
      But this my masculine usurped attire,
      Do not embrace me, till each circumstance, 235
      Of place, time, fortune, do cohere and jump
      That I am Viola, which to confirm
      I'll bring you to a captain in this town,
      Where lie my maiden weeds; by whose gentle help
      I was preserved – to serve this noble count. 240
      All the occurrence of my fortune since
      Hath been between this lady and this lord.

SEBASTIAN [To Olivia] So comes it, lady, you have been mistook.
      But nature to her bias drew in that.
      You would have been contracted to a maid; 245
      Nor are you therein, by my life, deceived;
      You are betrothed both to a maid and man.

ORSINO Be not amazed, right noble is his blood.
      If this be so – as yet the glass seems true –
      I shall have share in this most happy wreck. 250
      [To Viola] Boy, thou hast said to me a thousand times
      Thou never shouldst love woman like to me.

VIOLA And all those sayings will I overswear,
      And all those swearings keep as true in soul
      As doth that orbèd continent the fire 255
      That severs day from night.

ORSINO   Give me thy hand.
      And let me see thee in thy woman's weeds.

VIOLA The captain that did bring me first on shore
      Hath my maid's garments; he upon some action
      Is now in durance, at Malvolio's suit, 260
      A gentleman and follower of my lady's.

Feste brings Malvolio's letter. It reports Malvolio's suffering and his indignation. Olivia orders Malvolio to be brought in. She proposes a joint wedding celebration for the two couples at her house.

1 Handwriting reveals personality?

Some people believe that handwriting reveals character – do you? Write out Malvolio's letter (lines 282–90) in a style of handwriting which you think reflects his personality.

2 'He holds Belzebub at the stave's end'

Malvolio is fighting to keep the devil at a distance (as if with a long staff or rod), says Feste. Close your eyes and try to conjure up the picture the words produce in your mind. Talk together with other students about their images. Draw the picture you have in your mind.

3 Reading the letter (in threes)

Olivia won't allow Feste to read Malvolio's letter, because he puts on a mad voice. But how does Fabian read it, and how would Malvolio speak what he's written? Read lines 282–90:

- as Feste
- as Fabian
- as Malvolio.

4 Deliver

The word 'deliver' is used in three different ways in lines 271, 273 and 294. Work out the different meanings in each case.

---

enlarge release
much distract mad
most extracting frenzy madness
epistles/gospels letters/truths
  (and puns on religious meanings,
  see page 164)
skills not much doesn't matter
well edified satisfied

vox voice (Latin), style of speaking
perpend consider, pay attention
semblance appearance
leave my duty . . . unthought of
  go beyond my place as steward
crown th'alliance on't celebrate
  the double marriage

OLIVIA He shall enlarge him; fetch Malvolio hither.
        And yet, alas, now I remember me,
        They say, poor gentleman, he's much distract.

Enter CLOWN [FESTE], *with a letter, and* FABIAN

        A most extracting frenzy of mine own   265
        From my remembrance clearly banished his.
        How does he, sirrah?
FESTE Truly, madam, he holds Belzebub at the stave's end as well as
        a man in his case may do; h'as here writ a letter to you; I should
        have given't you today morning. But as a madman's epistles are no   270
        gospels, so it skills not much when they are delivered.
OLIVIA Open't and read it.
FESTE Look then to be well edified when the fool delivers the madman.
        [*Reads madly*] 'By the Lord, madam –'
OLIVIA How now, art thou mad?   275
FESTE No, madam, I do but read madness; and your ladyship will have
        it as it ought to be, you must allow *vox*.
OLIVIA Prithee read i'thy right wits.
FESTE So I do, madonna; but to read his right wits is to read thus.
        Therefore, perpend, my princess, and give ear.   280
OLIVIA [*To Fabian*] Read it you, sirrah.
FABIAN [*Reads*] 'By the Lord, madam, you wrong me, and the world
        shall know it. Though you have put me into darkness, and given
        your drunken cousin rule over me, yet have I the benefit of my
        senses as well as your ladyship. I have your own letter that induced 285
        me to the semblance I put on; with the which I doubt not but to
        do myself much right, or you much shame. Think of me as you
        please. I leave my duty a little unthought of and speak out of my
        injury.

                        The madly used Malvolio.'   290
OLIVIA Did he write this?
FESTE Ay, madam.
ORSINO This savours not much of distraction.
OLIVIA See him delivered, Fabian; bring him hither.

                                        [*Exit Fabian*]
        My lord, so please you, these things further thought on,   295
        To think me as well a sister as a wife,
        One day shall crown th'alliance on't, so please you,
        Here at my house, and at my proper cost.

Orsino proposes marriage to Viola. Malvolio shows Olivia the forged letter,
describes what has happened to him, and demands an explanation.
Olivia recognises that the letter is in Maria's handwriting.

1 'You are she!' (in small groups)

Can Olivia tell which twin is which? Could line 305 mean that Olivia
has looked away from the twins and now has to guess which is Viola?
Some people think the line cannot possibly have that interpretation.
Others feel strongly that it could.

Do you think Olivia has difficulty recognising which is Viola and
which is Sebastian? Take sides and argue for and against. Better still,
act out different versions of what happens as Olivia speaks line 305.
Which interpretation do you think is most appropriate to the mood of
the scene?

2 Sympathy for Malvolio? (in pairs)

Would you want Malvolio's appearance and way of speaking to win
the audience's sympathy for his mistreatment? Talk about how you
think Malvolio should enter and whether his manner has changed.
Then try out different ways of speaking lines 309–23, being:

a very angry
b very calm, dignified and reasoned
c close to tears
d utterly bewildered.

3 Should Malvolio glare at the Priest?

In one production, Malvolio glared at the Priest with great indignation as he spoke line 321. Give reasons why you think such a piece of
stage business is appropriate or not.

apt ready	**invention (line 312)** style
quits releases	**lighter people** servants
mettle nature	**geck and gull** fool and dupe
peruse read	**invention (line 323)** trick, deceit
Write from it write differently	**the character** my handwriting

ORSINO Madam, I am most apt t'embrace your offer.
  [*To Viola*] Your master quits you; and for your service
    done him,   300
  So much against the mettle of your sex,
  So far beneath your soft and tender breeding,
  And since you called me master for so long,
  Here is my hand; you shall from this time be
  Your master's mistress.
OLIVIA   Ah, sister, you are she!   305

          Enter [FABIAN *with*] MALVOLIO

ORSINO Is this the madman?
OLIVIA   Ay, my lord, this same.
  How now, Malvolio?
MALVOLIO   Madam, you have done me wrong,
  Notorious wrong.
OLIVIA   Have I, Malvolio? No.
MALVOLIO Lady, you have. Pray you, peruse that letter.
  You must not now deny it is your hand;   310
  Write from it, if you can, in hand, or phrase,
  Or say 'tis not your seal, not your invention.
  You can say none of this. Well, grant it then,
  And tell me, in the modesty of honour,
  Why you have given me such clear lights of favour,   315
  Bade me come smiling and cross-gartered to you,
  To put on yellow stockings, and to frown
  Upon Sir Toby, and the lighter people;
  And acting this in an obedient hope,
  Why have you suffered me to be imprisoned,   320
  Kept in a dark house, visited by the priest,
  And made the most notorious geck and gull,
  That e'er invention played on? Tell me, why?
OLIVIA Alas, Malvolio, this is not my writing,
  Though I confess much like the character.   325
  But, out of question, 'tis Maria's hand.
  And now I do bethink me, it was she
  First told me thou wast mad; then cam'st in smiling,
  And in such forms which here were presupposed
  Upon thee in the letter. Prithee, be content;   330

                        145

Fabian reveals the plot against Malvolio and announces that Sir Toby has married Maria. Feste teases Malvolio, who leaves swearing revenge. Orsino looks forward to his marriage to Viola.

1 Malvolio's revenge

'I'll be revenged on the whole pack of you!' Does Malvolio mean it – and does he get his revenge? Some people think that the line is a forewarning of the English Civil War, which took place forty years after *Twelfth Night* was written. The puritans seized power, closed the theatres, and attempted to end all frivolity and merrymaking.

a Write a short story or poem called 'Malvolio's revenge'.
b Decide how Malvolio speaks his final line: angrily, in tears, as a whisper, and so on.
c Turn to the list of characters on page 1. Consider each character in turn. What would be Malvolio's preferred revenge on each?

2 Olivia's final line – anger or sympathy?

In one production, Olivia was clearly very angry with Feste. She hit him as she spoke line 356. Do you think that such an action is in character with Olivia, and appropriate to the final moments of the play? Decide what you would advise Olivia to do at line 356.

3 Closing image (in small groups)

Everyone except Feste leaves the stage at line 365. Imagine you are directing the play. What atmosphere do you wish to create for the audience in these closing moments? A mood of harmony, with the characters pairing up happily as they leave? Or some other atmosphere that you could justify because of your view of the play as a whole? Work out how everyone except Feste leaves the stage. What about Antonio who has been a silent watcher for so long?

---

practice trick
shrewdly passed mischievously worked
grounds reasons
plaintiff accuser
Taint poison, contaminate

Upon some stubborn . . . him because we thought him stiff-necked and uncivil
importance insistence
baffled shamefully humiliated
convents calls us together
combination union, marriage

This practice hath most shrewdly passed upon thee;
But when we know the grounds, and authors of it,
Thou shalt be both the plaintiff and the judge
Of thine own cause.

FABIAN   Good madam, hear me speak,
        And let no quarrel, nor no brawl to come,   335
        Taint the condition of this present hour,
        Which I have wondered at. In hope it shall not,
        Most freely I confess, myself and Toby
        Set this device against Malvolio here,
        Upon some stubborn and uncourteous parts   340
        We had conceived against him. Maria writ
        The letter, at Sir Toby's great importance,
        In recompense whereof he hath married her.
        How with a sportful malice it was followed
        May rather pluck on laughter than revenge,   345
        If that the injuries be justly weighed,
        That have on both sides passed.

OLIVIA Alas, poor fool, how have they baffled thee!

FESTE   Why, 'Some are born great, some achieve greatness, and some
        have greatness thrown upon them.' I was one, sir, in this interlude,   350
        one Sir Topas, sir – but that's all one. 'By the Lord, fool, I am not
        mad.' But do you remember – 'Madam, why laugh you at such a
        barren rascal, and you smile not, he's gagged'? And thus the
        whirligig of time brings in his revenges.

MALVOLIO I'll be revenged on the whole pack of you!   [Exit]   355

OLIVIA He hath been most notoriously abused.

ORSINO Pursue him, and entreat him to a peace.
        He hath not told us of the captain yet.

                                                    [Exit Fabian]

        When that is known, and golden time convents,
        A solemn combination shall be made   360
        Of our dear souls. Meantime, sweet sister,
        We will not part from hence. Cesario, come –
        For so you shall be while you are a man,
        But when in other habits you are seen,
        Orsino's mistress, and his fancy's queen.   365

                                        Exeunt [all but Feste]

Feste, alone on stage, sings about growing up, about being tolerated in childhood, rejected in adulthood, unsuccessful in marriage, and drunk in old age. But nothing really matters, the actors will always try to please.

foolish thing child
toy trifle, triviality
man's estate manhood

swaggering blustering
tosspots drunkards

(Clown sings)

When that I was and-a little tiny boy,
　With hey, ho, the wind and the rain,
A foolish thing was but a toy,
　For the rain it raineth every day.

But when I came to man's estate,   370
　With hey, ho, the wind and the rain,
'Gainst knaves and thieves men shut their gate,
　For the rain it raineth every day.
But when I came, alas, to wive,
　With hey, ho, the wind and the rain,   375
By swaggering could I never thrive,
　For the rain it raineth every day.

But when I came unto my beds,
　With hey, ho, the wind and the rain,
With tosspots still 'had drunken heads,   380
　For the rain it raineth every day.

A great while ago the world begun,
　With hey, ho, the wind and the rain,
But that's all one, our play is done,
　And we'll strive to please you every day.   [*Exit*]   385

Looking back at the play
Activities for groups or individuals

1 The whirligig of time

Earlier in the play (1.3.34) Sir Toby spoke of 'the parish top', a whipping top used in play by adults. Now Feste plays his own variation on the notion that 'the wheel has come full circle', and uses the image of a child's whipping top ('whirligig'). Sketch out the plot of the play as a circular or spiral diagram with the title 'the whirligig of time'.

2 Happy ever after?

The play ends with news of one marriage (Sir Toby and Maria), and the promise of two to come in 'golden time' (Viola and Orsino, Olivia and Sebastian). What will happen to each? Choose one of the six characters, imagine you are he or she and write a chapter of your autobiography ten years later, in which you describe what's happened to you and the other couples.

3 Music: the food of love?

Twelfth Night is the only one of Shakespeare's plays that begins and ends with music. Identify each time music is played or sung, and talk together about what you think each occasion has to do with an aspect of music as the food of love.

4 The Captain

What happens to the Captain? He had been imprisoned on Malvolio's order. Write his story.

5 What's your view?

'That's all one.' Here's what one student wrote about Feste's line 384 at the end of Act 5:

> 'It puzzles me because it seems to mean "it doesn't matter". This seems to say that love and enjoyment aren't worth it, because time makes an end of everything. But surely the play is about life and happiness and love, and that's what matters?'

What would you say to her about her puzzlement?

6 Sympathy for Malvolio?

What is the attitude of each character towards Malvolio? Olivia seems to have sympathy for him ('poor fool' is probably spoken compassionately). But Feste taunts him with snatches of earlier lines. Consider each character in turn. Say, with reasons, how you think they feel towards Malvolio at the end of the play.

7 Feste's final song

On stage, the mood of Feste's final song is often sad and regretful. But when the play was performed in Shakespeare's own lifetime, Feste probably danced a jig (a merry dance) and sang in a lively, cheerful manner. Feste's mysterious song has been interpreted in very different ways. Which of the following descriptions do you think is the most appropriate?

'moving, poignant and uneven'
'sardonic and satirical'
'less cheerful than might be expected'
'meant as a cheerful conclusion'
'melancholy beauty'
'clumsy and tacked on'
'disturbing'
'haunting refrain'

What mood would you wish to create with these final words? Talk together about how you would stage the song. Act out your version.

8 Epilogues

At the end of Shakespeare's *As You Like It*, Rosalind, the main character, speaks directly to the audience. In *A Midsummer Night's Dream*, Puck does the same. So too does the King of France in *All's Well That Ends Well*. What if Shakespeare had chosen a character other than Feste to have the final word? Choose a character from the play and write and perform their epilogue.

9 Curtain call

In the last line of his song, Feste reminds the audience that they are not in Illyria – they are watching a play, an illusion, not real life. Take line 385 as the cue for the actors to stage their final curtain call to acknowledge the applause of the audience. How do they do it?

Twelfth Night

In Elizabethan times, the twelve days after Christmas up to Twelfth Night on 6 January (Epiphany) were traditionally a time of holiday and festival. It was a time for celebration and revelry, sometimes known as the 'Feast of Fools'. Normal behaviour and conventions could be suspended in this period of high jinks. Authority was up-ended. In universities, private houses and the Inns of Court (the law schools in London), a 'Lord of Misrule' was chosen (often a servant) who became, for a short period, master of the household. He (never she) organised dances, masques and make-believe activities.

All kinds of folly, pranks and deceptions were allowed in this topsy-turvy world of confusion and masquerades. A never-never land was created, remote from the normal daily world. Illusions, festivities and riotous madness set the mood. Commonsense and decorum went out of the window. Pleasure and madness flourished as people were released from their everyday inhibitions. Comedy and carnival, disguise and boisterous frivolity were the order of the day.

But Twelfth Night marked the end of both the Christmas holiday, and the holiday season. The next day it was back to the normality of hard work in the everyday world. The short time of pleasure was over. So 6 January was tinged with sadness, as the Christmas decorations were taken down and the festivities ended.

The brief period of festivity allowed people to do as they pleased, and to indulge their fantasies. For a short time, servants could order their masters about. Today, a relic of this tradition is the custom in the Army for officers to serve Christmas dinner to the soldiers. But the major function of the twelve days was to remind the underdogs where power really lay, and that the normal hierarchy would and must be obeyed after the short holiday.

a Talk about what might happen if a 'Lord of Misrule' was elected for a day in your school or college. What would you do if you were elected?

b Find out about modern periods of festivity such as the Notting Hill carnival, *mardi gras* festivals in New Orleans and Rio de Janeiro, and the Munich Oktoberfest. Do you think they are like the Feast of Fools?

The Bean-King by Jacob Jordaens (1642). The custom of appointing a Lord of Misrule from Christmas Day to Twelfth Night was widespread in Europe for many centuries. Its origins lay in the Kalends or Saturnalia of ancient Rome, a time when slaves and masters changed places, and a mock king ruled a topsy-turvy world. At the Universities of Oxford and Cambridge, he was known as 'King of the Kingdom of the Bean', a title also used in Holland and Germany. When the University of Cambridge unsuccessfully tried to suppress the Bean-King and his revelry in 1646, 'some grave Governors mentioned the good use thereof, because thereby, in twelve days, they more discover the dispositions of Scholars than in twelve months before'.

Illyria

Shakespeare's Illyria, a never-never land of make-believe and illusion, exists under many names: Utopia, the Big Rock Candy Mountain, fairyland, Xanadu, Arcadia, the Land of Cockaigne, Shangri La, New Atlantis, Blue Remembered Hills, Dreamland. It is an enchanted land where happiness is truly possible; a fictitious world of romance, full of magical possibilities, thrilling and exotic, where anything can happen, but the result will be joy and harmony.

In other words, it's a state of mind, not the coast of Croatia and Albania on the Adriatic Sea. It is a world which exists in the imagination, a world in which characters are changed by experience. Shakespeare created similar worlds in his other plays: the Forest of Arden (*As You Like It*), the wood outside Athens (*A Midsummer Night's Dream*), Belmont (*The Merchant of Venice*), Ephesus (*The Comedy of Errors*). In these exotic locations of Shakespeare's comedies, confusions, errors and mistakes are made, but happiness and marriage result.

Illyria is a capricious world of disguise and mistaken identity. Language itself is unreliable – words slip and slide into confusion. Fantasy and everyday life rub shoulders – a fairy-tale Duke inhabits the same world as the earthy Sir Toby Belch, a very English drunkard. Everything is untrustworthy and larger than life. Commonsense is mocked, and nothing is quite what it seems. Folly abounds – one of the chief characters, Feste, is called 'the Fool'. The threat of madness is common (the word 'mad' occurs more times in *Twelfth Night* than in any other play by Shakespeare). Much madness is to do with love, but Malvolio is almost driven to real madness.

But Illyria, for all its untrustworthiness, is a secure place. Brother finds sister, lovers will marry. Illusions are the way to find truth, and time will achieve a happy ending for most, but not all, of the characters. Some characters finish up with their heart's desire – or think they do.

The subtitle of the play, *What You Will*, was a common catchphrase in Shakespeare's time. Perhaps it says to the audience: 'make of it what you like, it's make-believe, but don't take it too seriously, because nothing is of consequence'.

A modern Illyria? Disney World, where fantasy rules.

Create your own Illyria

a Make a display (a collage, photo-montage, or other illustration) to show your view of Illyria. Include quotations from the play.

b 'There's no such place as Illyria.'
   'Oh yes there is!'
   Take sides and argue for each claim.

What kind of play is *Twelfth Night?*

Twelfth Night does not have a single 'correct' meaning. Like all of Shakespeare's plays, it can be interpreted in different ways. To help you make up your own mind about what kind of play it is, consider each of the following perspectives on the play:

1 A comedy: 'cakes and ale'

A very amusing and charming play, sunny and always enjoyable. Filled with innocent laughter and preposterous situations, it has a happy ending which restores harmony to the temporary confusion of Illyria. All the characters are likeable and funny, Sir Toby is a lovable rogue, and even Malvolio has his comic appeal, especially when he gets what he deserves at the play's end. The whole play is simply a delightful entertainment which must never be taken seriously.

2 The triumph of love: 'love-thoughts lie rich'

The play is all about love in its many forms, but with true love winning through at the end. Olivia and Orsino are the mourning lady and romantic hero of literary convention. Their selfish, self-centred love is transformed to genuine love by the constancy and integrity of Viola, the embodiment of true and faithful love. Even Sir Toby finds love of a sort with Maria, and Sir Andrew and Malvolio learn that playing at love, or self-love, is not enough.

3 A poignant, elegiac play: 'youth's a stuff will not endure'

The play is sentimental and wistful. The humour, apart from Sir Toby's coarseness, is witty and tender. There are many moving moments as Viola speaks her beautiful and poignant lines of love. She longs for a fulfilment which, until the end of the play, is out of her grasp. The elegiac note is struck constantly with the many references to time ('the clock upbraids me with the waste of time'), and in the sound of the ever-changing sea echoing through the play. Feste's songs are reminders that love, like life, will end. The play is a plea for a quiet acceptance of the inevitable, and for finding solace in whatever temporary happiness we can grasp.

4 Troubling undertones: 'I'll be revenged on the whole pack of you!'

An upsetting play which seems light and amusing on the surface, yet has dark and harsh depths. It is an uneasy play about outsiders who lose, Antonio is left sad and alone at the end. Malvolio leaves seeking revenge, not reconciliation. Orsino and Olivia are smug and self-centred. They learn nothing, and are just the same at the play's end as at the beginning. Illyria is an oppressive society where no one at the top works. It breeds self-indulgence in idle aristocrats. Maria and her fellow-conspirators are prompted by ill-will towards Malvolio. The cruel baiting of Malvolio is little more than theatre as blood sport. Malvolio is a scapegoat, because Illyria needs him as someone to punish for the misdeeds of society. The play is a cruel satire which foreshadows Shakespeare's tragedies. It forecasts the English Civil War, which will see the triumph of the puritans and the extinguishing of theatre and merriment.

5 An elusive play: 'nothing that is so is so'

Twelfth Night is like quicksilver (mercury), elusive and impossible to grasp. It is always taking different shapes and meanings – a strange mixture, sometimes funny, sometimes sad. It contains both romance and revenge, and you can never be sure if love really triumphs, or if revenge and uncertainty will follow. It is a kaleidoscope of characters and events, all with mysterious sides to them. And the ending can be played any way you like!

6 An actor's play: 'if this were played upon a stage . . .'

Twelfth Night is a play which revels in its own theatricality, delighting in double-dealing, word-play and illusion. Viola acts the part of a boy, Malvolio acts the part of a deluded lover. The meaning of words and the relationships between people are unstable and unsure. Nothing is quite what it seems. A concern with the difference between appearance and reality runs all through the play, most notably in Viola's disguise as a boy, Cesario. It is a golden opportunity for actors to explore the slipperiness of language, and the dramatic irony which arises from disguise and mistaken identity.

Find two or three quotations from the play to illustrate each of the above perspectives. Then write a paragraph giving your own view of *Twelfth Night*.

Love in *Twelfth Night*

The very first line announces that love will be a central theme of the play: 'If music be the food of love, play on'. Shakespeare presents a rich variety of types of love in *Twelfth Night*.

The modern, western idea is that individuals fall in love and marry simply for personal qualities. In Elizabethan England, that belief was not held by everyone. Among the nobility and rich families, marriages were often arranged. Personal choice was unimportant, and marriage of sons and daughters would extend or maintain wealth, land and power. The economic reality of arranged marriages was overlaid by two beliefs much written about in stories and plays:

> *Courtly love* Women were 'put on a pedestal' and worshipped from afar as unattainable goddesses. Only by long devotion, many trials and much suffering, could a man win his ideal woman, the 'fair, cruel maid' of literature. Such love was sexless and idealised. In reality, it usually meant that men (like Orsino) were in love with the idea of love itself.

> *Romantic love* This was also idealised and unsexual, but it included 'love at first sight', and marriage was its natural result.

Both kinds of love produced 'the melancholy lover', the man who suffered for his love. He sighed and longed for the woman he adored. She was always difficult to attain. Such kinds of love were the product of masculine ideology: women treated merely as possessions. They might be hard to obtain, but they were possessions nevertheless.

Shakespeare drew heavily upon these conventions of love. He read about them in the literature of Elizabethan England. His genius lay in being able to mock the conventions and to suggest that love could be a partnership of equals. He could see that women's desires and capacity for feeling were on equal terms with men's, not inferior to them. In all his comedies, Shakespeare portrays intelligent and spirited women who more than hold their own in the love battles of the sexes. But even Viola, for all her clear-sightedness, falls head over heels in love with Orsino. Her love seems to make her blind to the less attractive side of his nature.

Orsino: self-indulgent love?

Orsino is Shakespeare's presentation of the melancholy lover, in love with the idea of love itself. Consider each of the following statements in turn, and say whether or not you think they give you a true insight into his personality:

he is changeable and moody ('Enough; no more')

he wallows in his emotions ('Love-thoughts lie rich')

he talks incessantly of love ('O spirit of love')

he thinks his love greater than anyone else's ('my love more noble than the world')

he considers himself an authority on love ('such as I am all true lovers are')

he speaks the language of exaggeration ('give me excess of it', 'as hungry as the sea')

he links love with sickness ('sicken and so die')

he thinks Olivia will totally submit to his love ('one selfsame king')

he worships Olivia like a goddess ('now heaven walks on earth')

he does not woo Olivia himself, but sends messengers

he threatens to murder Viola-Cesario

he switches his love abruptly from Olivia to Viola

his last words ('his fancy's queen') are not true love, but romantic fantasy – he substitutes one dream for another.

Olivia: self-denying, self-deceiving love?

Olivia has vowed to shut herself away from the world for seven years for love of her dead brother. She speedily breaks that vow. Her love, like Orsino's, is often described as 'sentimental':

she thinks highly of her own good looks ('Is't not well done?')

she is quickly infatuated by Viola-Cesario's appearance ('Not so fast! Soft, soft!')

she constantly beseeches Viola-Cesario to visit her

she marries Sebastian without recognising he is not Viola-Cesario

she equates love with sickness ('Even so quickly may one catch the plague?').

Talk together about whether or not Olivia's actions can be explained because she has been protected from the world by her father and brother. Does she reject Orsino's advances because she suspects that he, like her male relatives, will simply dominate her?

Malvolio: self-love?

'O you are sick of self-love, Malvolio.' Olivia's accusation sums up the traditional view of Malvolio:

he is highly critical of people below him

he is disdainful towards Viola when returning the ring

he is intolerant of Sir Toby's merrymaking

he has secret fantasies that Olivia loves him

his self-conceit causes him to fall easily into the trap set for him

he does not realise how ridiculous he looks, smiling and cross-gartered

he cannot forgive, but thinks only of revenge.

Are there ways of acting Malvolio so that he does not come over as a vain and pompous hypocrite? Make a list of all the ways you could present him on stage to challenge the stereotype of a conceited, self-loving killjoy.

Viola: selfless love?

Virtually all interpretations agree that Viola represents true love in the play. She is not self-seeking, but self-sacrificing. She speaks simply and directly about her love in language which is not affected, but sincere. Her love for Orsino is constant, deep and pure:

she remains true to Orsino throughout the play

she unquestioningly carries out Orsino's orders to woo Olivia

she speaks the most moving and sincere lines about love in the play

she tells Olivia what genuine love really is like

she is not interested in status, but in persons

she is willing to die for love when Orsino threatens her

her love ensures that Olivia and Orsino turn away from self-indulgent and self-deceiving love.

But there are some puzzling aspects to Viola's love. Talk together about your views on the following:

a Why does she say about Orsino 'he was a bachelor then'?

b What does she see in Orsino? Most writers on the play see him as a self-centred, ambitious poseur who doesn't know what true love really is.

Sir Andrew Aguecheek: a secret love?

Sir Andrew is almost always presented on stage as being foolish, with no chance at all of winning Olivia's love. But he has one of the most endearing lines in the play: 'I was adored once too'. Do you think there is more to Sir Andrew than conventional interpretations suggest? Write the story of Sir Andrew's long-ago secret romance when he was 'adored'.

Sir Toby and Maria: sex or soul mates?

Sir Toby marries Maria just before the end of the play. Talk about what you think draws them together. If it's love, what kind of love?

Antonio: love as true friendship?

Antonio's love ('more sharp than filed steel') makes him follow Sebastian without thought of his own safety. Some critics see his love as the only really true love in the play. Others suspect that his love for Sebastian might be homosexual. What's your view?

Love as a disease

Make a list of as many references as you can find in the play which link or equate love with sickness or disease. For example, in Act 1 Scene 1: 'sicken' (line 3), 'falls into abatement' (line 13), 'pestilence' (line 20), 'killed' (line 36).

A rank order of love?

Whose love is genuine and whose is not? Draw a line about twelve centimetres long. Label one end 'True love', and the other end 'Insincere love'. Rank every character in order along the line.

Will love last?

At the end of the play, some characters 'pair up'. Consider each couple in turn and talk together about whether or not you think their love will last.

Men or women: whose love is stronger?

Orsino says that men's love is 'more giddy and unfirm' than women's love (Act 2 Scene 4, lines 31–3). But a few minutes later, he says his love is stronger than any woman's (lines 89–92)! Talk together about which of Orsino's claims you agree with, or whether you think that men's and women's loves are equally strong – or weak!

Illyria: Shakespeare's England

Like all writers, Shakespeare reflected in his plays the world he knew. Illyria sounds like a faraway place – Orsino, Antonio and Malvolio are 'un-English' names (unlike Sir Toby, Sir Andrew and 'Mistress Mary'). But *Twelfth Night* is full of the customs, sights and sounds of Elizabethan England:

Hunting and field sports hounds, bird-bolts, beagle, stone-bow, staniel, cold scent, sowter, fox, haggard, feather, woodcock, gin, unmuzzled, whipstock.

Eating and drinking buttery-bar, canary, sack, beef, alehouse, tosspots, pickled herring.

Songs and dances jig, galliard, coranto, caper, back-trick, sink-a-pace, catch, cantons, tabor, 'hold thy peace'.

The countryside squash, peascod, codling, turkey-cock, dormouse, grey capilet, oxen and wainropes, bawcock, chuck, biddy, sheriff's post, orchard, box-tree.

Familiar words or phrases It's all one, Peg-a-Ramsey, cudgel, leman (sweetheart), cheveril glove, westward ho, the old Vice, asshead, coxcomb, knave, gull, what you will, coz, swabber, sneck up.

Occupations coziers, tinkers, weavers, stewards, spinsters (who spin flax on a distaff), knitters, grand jurymen, bumbailey, master crowner (coroner), parson, curate, Dick Surgeon, coistrill, groom.

Current affairs puritan, Brownist, Yeomen of the wardrobe, Mistress Mall's picture, Lady of the Strachy, Dutchman's beard, the new map of the Indies, the sophy.

Places and customs south suburbs, the Elephant, St Bennet, the great bed of Ware, parish top, inventories, tray-trip, cherry-pit, acqua-vitae, bear-baiting.

Clothes gaskins, points, changeable taffeta, branched velvet gown, yellow stockings, cross-gartered.

- Identify in the script as many of the above as you can.
- Talk together about whether you think that writers inevitably reflect in their work the beliefs, values and customs of their own times.

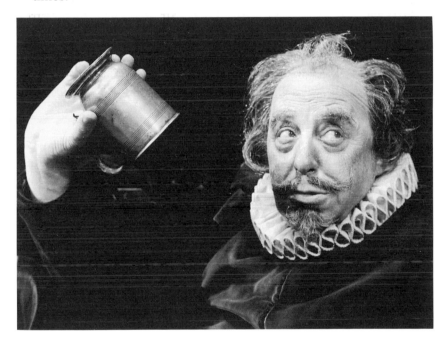

Sir Toby Belch – an Englishman in Illyria?

The language of *Twelfth Night*

1 Imagery

Twelfth Night is full of imagery: words or phrases which conjure up emotionally-laden pictures in the mind. Orsino's language in Act 1 Scene 1 contains a series of images which recur through the play: music, death, the sea, hunting, disease ('pestilence'), love and flowers. Choose one image, find as many uses of it in the play as you can, and work out a vivid and effective way of displaying your findings (for example, an illustrated 'spider diagram').

2 Feste: 'her corrupter of words'

Feste delights in word-play. He makes puns (where the same sound or word has different meanings), engages in repartee (quick-fire exchanges), invents mock-logical arguments ('this simple syllogism'), makes up high-sounding but fake names ('Quinapalus', 'the old hermit of Prague'), offers mock-religious advice ('Well, God give them wisdom that have it'), and always seizes any opportunity to create both sense and nonsense from words. Follow Feste through the play and collect examples of his different types of word-play.

3 Dramatic irony

Dramatic irony is present when the audience knows something which a character on stage does not. For example, when Viola says 'I am not what I am', Olivia is unaware of the full significance of Viola's words, whereas Viola and the audience realise what is really meant, namely that Viola is female. The emphasis on disguise in *Twelfth Night* means that the play is full of dramatic irony – a source of great amusement! Identify one example of dramatic irony in each act.

4 Soliloquies and asides

A soliloquy is spoken by a character who is alone (or assumes he or she is alone) on stage. An aside is a comment which a character makes, unheard by other characters on stage. Soliloquies and asides usually reveal the true thoughts and feelings of a character. Find the soliloquies and asides spoken by Viola, Olivia and Malvolio. Choose one, and work out a way of presenting it as dramatically as possible.

5 Key words

The words 'love' and 'madness' echo through the play. Identify how often each word is used, and who uses it. Display your findings in as powerful a way as possible.

6 Prose and verse

About two-thirds of the play is written in prose. As a general rule, Shakespeare's high-status characters speak verse, and low-status characters speak prose. But that rule is often broken in *Twelfth Night*. Viola frequently switches from verse to prose, and Sir Toby and Sir Andrew always use prose. So, a better general rule for *Twelfth Night* is that prose is the style for comic scenes and characters, and verse is the style for lovers and for 'serious' moments. But remember, Shakespeare never sticks rigidly to any rule!

- Glance quickly over each scene in the play, and make a list showing which are mainly in verse, and which are mainly in prose. Suggest why.
- Follow Viola through the play identifying where she speaks verse, where prose. Give reasons for her type of speech at each of the various points. Remember that 'poetry' (verse) is the traditional language of love.
- Malvolio and Fabian speak mainly prose. But in Act 5 they have some lines in verse. Read the lines aloud, and suggest why Shakespeare gives them verse at these moments.

7 Songs

Make a list of all the songs or snatches of songs in the play. Write a sentence alongside each, suggesting how the song echoes the mood of the scene in which it is sung. For example, 'Come away, come away, death' echoes Orsino's melancholy mood in Act 2 Scene 4.

8 Images from mythology

Act 1 Scene 2 contains the first of many images from Greek and Latin mythology in the play: 'Elysium' and 'Arion on the dolphin's back'. Other examples are Diana (page 19), Vulcan (page 129), Jove (pages 25, 62, 67, 73 and 93), Mercury (page 23), Penthesilea (page 49), Lucrece (page 63) and Lethe (page 113). You will find brief explanations of each at appropriate points in the script. Take one example and write about how you think it helps to enrich the meaning of what is being said where it is used.

Staging *Twelfth Night*

A performance of the play was first recorded by John Manningham, a barrister. He wrote in his diary that he saw *Twelve Night or What you Will*, on 2 February 1602 in the Middle Temple of the Inns of Court in London. He said it had: 'good practice in it to make the steward believe his lady widow was in love with him, by counterfeiting a letter'. Manningham thought it was much like Shakespeare's *The Comedy of Errors*, which also involves shipwrecked twins and mistaken identity.

Shakespeare probably took the idea of his play from an English adaptation of an Italian story, but he made significant alterations. In the original, the sea-captain was a villain, Viola was imprisoned by the Duke, and Olivia has a child by Sebastian. Shakespeare invented the Sir Toby subplot. He drew on his earlier plays in which women dressed as men (*Two Gentlemen of Verona*, *The Merchant of Venice*, *As You Like It*). He must have also recalled the success of his 'ship-wrecked twins' and 'strangers in town' play, *The Comedy of Errors*.

Right from the play's first performance, Malvolio seized the imagination of audiences. In 1632, King Charles I wrote 'Malvolio' against the title of the play in the collection of Shakespeare's plays which he owned. Perhaps Malvolio's revenge is that he has turned out to be the best-remembered character in the play!

In 1660, the diarist Samuel Pepys saw the play three times. He thought it 'silly', and could not see the point of the title. The play fell from favour for almost eighty years after Pepys saw it, but other playwrights repeatedly drew on it as a source of ideas and language for their own plays.

After its revival in 1741, *Twelfth Night* became increasingly popular. Many leading actors chose to play Malvolio. His 'darkened room' scene was played in a range of styles from tragedy to farce. In the nineteenth century, it became fashionable to add musical scenes filled with spectacle and festivity – some productions were virtually operas! Sebastian, Olivia and Viola often sang, and Viola was sometimes played like a hearty and enthusiastic principal boy in a pantomime. The whole company would join in a song and dance at the play's end.

In the twentieth century, productions have moved away from elaborate spectacle. The concern has been to explore a complex variety of moods through close attention to language and characterisation. One Malvolio left the stage apparently intent on suicide. Another gave his final words such evil undertones that it completely changed the comic mood. Yet another Malvolio bore a striking resemblance to Shakespeare. In contrast with nineteenth-century productions, Olivia is now often played as a young woman, and Feste as a much older Fool.

Many modern productions stress the autumnal, elegiac mood of the play (see page 156). They suggest that fertility and romantic idyll will soon give way to decay and winter. There is a growing trend for modern productions to portray Illyria as a society undergoing change. So Illyria is set as a feudal, male-dominated society, exercising control through licensed foolery. But it is threatened by a more modern efficient society, characterised by the 'new man', the self-made, humourless Malvolio. He is impatient with the old order, and intolerant of fun and festivity. Such productions tend to see the play giving a forewarning of the class struggle to come, in the English Civil War of 1642–60 and the closure of the theatres.

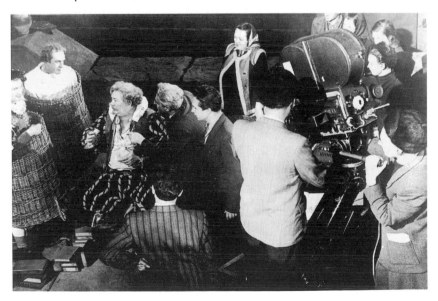

Filming *Twelfth Night* in 1955. A Russian camera crew prepares to film a scene. Can you guess which scene they are about to shoot?

Stage your own production of *Twelfth Night*

Talk together about the period and place in which you will set your play: a Mediterranean island? an Elizabethan country house? a 'timeless' setting? Then choose one or more of the following activities. Your finished assignment can be a file of drawings, notes and suggestions, or an active presentation.

- Design the set – how can it be used for particular scenes?
- Design the costumes.
- Design the publicity poster – make people want to see your play!
- Design the programme – think about layout, content and the number of pages you will need.
- Write character notes to help the actors.
- Work out a five-minute presentation to show potential sponsors.

Visit a production of *Twelfth Night*

Shakespeare wrote *Twelfth Night* to be acted, watched and enjoyed – not to be studied for examinations! So visit a live performance! Prepare for a school party visit through one or more of the following:

- Everyone chooses a character (or an incident or scene) to watch especially closely. Write down your expectations before you go. Report back to the class on how your expectations for 'your' character or scene were fulfilled or challenged.
- Choose your favourite line in the play. Listen carefully to how it is spoken. Does it add to your understanding?
- Your teacher will probably be able to provide one or two published reviews of the production. Talk together about whether you should read the reviews before or after you see the play for yourself. After the visit, decide how far you agree or disagree with the reviews.
- Write your own review. Don't think you have to copy the style of professional reviewers. Your review should record your own impressions of what you actually saw and heard, and your feelings about the production.

Two points to remember:

1 Preparation is always valuable, but too much preparation can kill the enjoyment of a theatre visit. So talk together with your teacher about how much preparation to do.

2 Every production is different. There's no such thing as a single right way to 'do' Shakespeare. But you might think that there are 'wrong' ways!

Who's who?

Below are some descriptions of the major characters: Orsino, Olivia, Viola, Malvolio, Sir Toby, Sir Andrew, Feste, Maria and Sebastian. For each character, select ten appropriate words. Some words will apply to more than one character. Remember, Shakespeare's characters are complex figures, with a mixture of personal qualities.

absurd	earthy	naïve	self-satisfied
acquisitive	egotistical	noble	self-willed
affected	emotional	officious	sensitive
affectionate	envious	oily	sentimental
anarchic	exquisite	opportunistic	sexy
anguished	fanciful		shrewd
appealing	fatuous	parasitical	silly
arrogant	foolish	passionate	sincere
austere	frank	patronising	slippery
bawdy	funny	pompous	smug
beguiled		practical	snobbish
bewildered	generous	priggish	sourpuss
bitter	genuine	proud	spoilsport
boisterous	good-humoured	quarrelsome	superficial
bold	honest	rational	susceptible
bully	hot-headed	realistic	tender
cheerful	humourless	repressed	tolerant
clear-sighted	hypocritical	resilient	two-faced
clever	imaginative	resourceful	unctuous
cold	immature	ridiculous	unforgiving
compassionate	impulsive	romantic	unheroic
complacent	inadequate	rude	unsympathetic
conceited	independent	rumbustious	vain
condescending	indolent	satirical	vengeful
constant	inexperienced	self-controlled	victimiser
courageous	intelligent	self-indulgent	vivacious
cowardly	intolerant	selfish	vulnerable
cruel	ironic	selfless	warm
cunning	killjoy	self-opinionated	well-balanced
cynical	malleable		wet blanket
determined	melancholy		witty
drunkard	mischief-maker		
dupe	mocking		
	moody		

Activities

1 The Fool

Fools were often employed in the palaces of royalty or noble families. Although they had the title of 'fool' (or jester or clown), they were much more intelligent than foolish ('a witty fool'). Their job was not simply to provide amusement, but to make critical comment on contemporary behaviour. An 'allowed fool' was able to say what he thought. No punishment would follow: 'there's no slander in an allowed fool'.

Feste is employed by Olivia, and was a favourite of her father. He gets on well with Sir Toby, and is just as much at home at Duke Orsino's. Feste is very much his own man, moving easily between all levels of society in Illyria. Only Malvolio dislikes him – for which Feste extracts revenge. Try some or all of the following activities:

a Write a list of words to describe Feste's character.
b Think about one or two of your favourite comedians. How are they like or unlike Feste?
c Talk together about whether you think there are modern equivalents of 'allowed fools' in society at large or in your own circle.
d What do you make of the student who came to school very scruffily dressed in old, dirty clothes? He argued that he was only following the instructions in the school handbook: 'school uniform must be worn' ('worn' can mean frayed, old). Would this kind of 'fool' be 'allowed' in your school or college?
e Research in the library to find out more about professional fools and jesters of the Elizabethan period.

2 A director talks to the cast

You are a director about to begin rehearsing a production of *Twelfth Night*. Prepare a short talk to give to the cast on your first meeting.

3 Malvolio's problem

You've been called out of bed to stop a noisy party downstairs. Improvise!

4 A break in performance

If you were putting on the play, where would you place the interval – and why?

5 The settings of the play

No one really knows where Shakespeare intended to set each scene. Turn back to the beginning of each scene and decide if you agree with the locations suggested. If not, propose your own setting, giving reasons for your choice.

6 Consider the characters

Turn to the list of characters on page 1. Consider each character in turn:

a Talk together about how much, and in what ways they have changed by the end of the play. Do you think some characters have not changed at all?
b Rank each character in order of social class.
c Rank them in order of (1) age, (2) emotional maturity.
d Write a sentence for each character which begins: 'What I want most is . . .'

7 Orsino

In 1601, an Italian nobleman, Don Virginio Orsino, Duke of Bracciano, visited Queen Elizabeth I in London. Is that where Shakespeare found the inspiration for Orsino's name? Take parts and role-play a discussion between Shakespeare and his fellow actors. One actor says: 'Look, it seems to me that you've made Orsino a conceited, moody, self-centred, affected, lovesick twerp. The Queen and the Duke are going to be mightily offended!' What does Shakespeare reply?

8 Start with the shipwreck?

Some productions begin the play with a scene of the shipwreck and Viola's landing on the coast of Illyria (that is, beginning with Scene 2, followed by Scene 1). Debate the merits and demerits of opening the play in that way.

9 No villains

'There are no villains in *Twelfth Night*.' Do you agree?

William Shakespeare 1564–1616

1564 Born Stratford-upon-Avon, eldest son of John and Mary Shakespeare.
1582 Marries Anne Hathaway of Shottery, near Stratford.
1583 Daughter, Susanna, born.
1585 Twins, son and daughter, Hamnet and Judith, born.
1592 First mention of Shakespeare in London. Robert Greene, another playwright, describes Shakespeare as 'an upstart crow beautified with our feathers . . .'. Greene seems to have been jealous of Shakespeare. He mocked Shakespeare's name, calling him 'the only Shake-scene in the country' (presumably because Shakespeare was writing successful plays).
1595 A shareholder in 'The Lord Chamberlain's Men', an acting company that becomes extremely popular.
1596 Son Hamnet dies, aged eleven.
     Father, John, granted arms (acknowledged as a gentleman).
1597 Buys New Place, the grandest house in Stratford.
1598 Acts in Ben Jonson's *Every Man in His Humour*.
1599 Globe Theatre opens on Bankside. Performances in the open air.
1601 Father, John, dies.
1603 James I grants Shakespeare's company a royal patent: 'The Lord Chamberlain's Men' become 'The King's Men' and play about twelve performances each year at court.
1607 Daughter, Susanna, marries Dr John Hall.
1608 Mother, Mary, dies.
1609 'The King's Men' begin performing indoors at Blackfriars Theatre.
1610 Probably returns from London to live in Stratford.
1616 Daughter, Judith, marries Thomas Quiney.
     Dies. Buried in Holy Trinity Church, Stratford-upon-Avon.

The plays and poems
(no one knows exactly when he wrote each play)

1589–1595 *The Two Gentlemen of Verona, The Taming of the Shrew, First, Second and Third Parts of King Henry VI, Titus Andronicus, King Richard III, The Comedy of Errors, Love's Labour's Lost, A Midsummer Night's Dream, Romeo and Juliet, King Richard II* (and the long poems *Venus and Adonis* and *The Rape of Lucrece*).

1596–1599 *King John, The Merchant of Venice, First and Second Parts of King Henry IV, The Merry Wives of Windsor, Much Ado About Nothing, King Henry V, Julius Caesar* (and probably the *Sonnets*).

1600–1605 *As You Like It, Hamlet, Twelfth Night, Troilus and Cressida, Measure for Measure, Othello, All's Well That Ends Well, Timon of Athens, King Lear.*

1606–1611 *Macbeth, Antony and Cleopatra, Pericles, Coriolanus, The Winter's Tale, Cymbeline, The Tempest.*

1613 *King Henry VIII, The Two Noble Kinsmen* (both probably with John Fletcher).

1623 Shakespeare's plays published as a collection (now called the First Folio).